REFLECTIO

In the name of Allāh,

Most Gracious, Most Merciful.

All praise be to Allāh, Lord of the Worlds, and peace and blessings be upon His Messenger Muḥammad, Mercy to the Worlds

REFLECTIONS OF PEARLS

A CONCISE & COMPREHENSIVE COLLECTION OF PROPHETIC INVOCATIONS & PRAYERS

Arabic Text with English Translation & Transliteration

INAM UDDIN &
ABDUR-RAHMAN IBN YUSUF MANGERA

White Thread
PRESS

1st Edition 1994. 2nd Edition 1996. 3rd Edition April 2005.
4th Edition November 2012. Reprint Mar 2016, Jul 2018, Feb 2020, Aug 2021.

ISBN 978-0-9728358-5-5

Published by:
White Thread Press
WT Press Limited, London, UK
www.whitethreadpress.com

Distributed in the UK by Azhar Academy Ltd. London
www.azharacademy.com

Library of Congress Cataloging-in-Publication Data

Uddin, Inam.
Reflections of pearls : a concise & comprehensive collection of prophetic invocations & prayers : Arabic text with English translation and transliteration / Inam Uddin & Abdur-Rahman ibn Yusuf.—3rd ed.
p. cm.
English and Arabic.
Includes bibliographical references.
ISBN 0-9728358-5-7 (softcover : alk. paper)
1. Islam—Prayer-books and devotions—English. 2. Islam—Prayer-books and devotions—Arabic. I. Ibn Yusuf, Abdur-Rahman, 1974- II. Title.
BP183.3.U33 2005
297.3'824—dc22

2005002739

♾ Printed and bound in Turkey on acid-free paper.
The paper used in this book meets the minimum requirement of ANSI/NISO Z39.48-1992 (R 1997) (Permanence of Paper). The binding material has been chosen for strength and durability.

Cover image of Alcazar, Seville, by F Poncelet
Book design and typography by ARM
Cover design by Farooq Ahmad

For Shaykh
Hashim Patel who
taught us the Sunan of
Imām Abū Dāwūd and
inspired us with his advice
and wisdom

TRANSLITERATION KEY

ء (أ إ)	' (A slight catch in the breath. It is also used to indicate where the *hamza* has been dropped from the beginning of a word.)
ا	a, ā
ب	b
ت	t
ث	th (Should be pronounced as the *th* in *thin* or *thirst*.)
ج	j
ح	ḥ (Tensely breathed *h* sound.)
خ	kh (Pronounced like the *ch* in Scottish *loch* with the mouth hollowed to produce a full sound.)
د	d
ذ	dh (Should be pronounced as the *th* in *this* or *that*.)
ر	r
ز	z
س	s
ش	sh
ص	ṣ (A heavy *s* pronounced far back in the mouth with the mouth hollowed to produce a full sound.)
ض	ḍ (A heavy *d/dh* pronounced far back in the mouth with the mouth hollowed to produce a full sound.)
ط	ṭ (A heavy *t* pronounced far back in the mouth with the mouth hollowed to produce a full sound.)
ظ	ẓ (A heavy *dh* pronounced far back in the mouth with the mouth hollowed to produce a full sound.)
ع	ʿ, ʿa, ʿi, ʿu (Pronounced from the throat.)
غ	gh (Pronounced like a throaty French *r* with the mouth hollowed to produce a full sound.)
ف	f
ق	q (A guttural *q* sound with the mouth hollowed to produce a full sound.)
ك	k
ل	l
م	m
ن	n
و	w, ū, u.
ه	h
ي	y, ī, i
ﷺ	Used following the mention of the Messenger Muḥammad, translated as, "May Allāh bless him and give him peace."
ﷷ	Used following the mention of a Prophet or Messenger of Allāh, translated as, "May the peace of Allāh be upon him."
ؓ	Used following the mention of a Companion of the Messenger, translated as, "May Allāh be pleased with him."
ؓ	Used following the mention of more than one Companion of the Messenger (and also after a female Companion in this work for lack of an appropriate glyph), translated as, "May Allāh be pleased with them."

The *duʿās* in this book have been transliterated using a convention different from the standard used for transliterating Arabic terms in the main text. Hence, words are represented as they should be pronounced and the interword connections are transliterated according to the following guidelines:

(1) Silent *hamzas* (*waṣl*) have been omitted and replaced with an apostrophe ('). In this case, the word before it should be connected to the letter after the apostrophe; e.g., *wa 'l-māli.*

(2) Commas have been added to indicate appropriate places of pause. Letters enclosed in parentheses are not read when pausing; e.g., *fī khayr(in).*

(3) In instances where there is elision (*idgham*) between two words, the words are transliterated in their elided forms; e.g., *wāsi-ʿaw wa shifā'am min.* However, in some cases, to facilitate a pause, the non-elided form is shown, followed by the elided form in square brackets; e.g., *jadīdan[w], wa.* In this example, the [*w*] replaces *n* only when continuing.

CONTENTS

FOREWORD

In the name of Allāh, the Beneficent, the Merciful. All praise is due to Allāh, the One, the Mighty Administrator of all worldly affairs, who favored us with His faith and bequeathed upon us blessings that enabled us to worship Him and duly thank Him. Peace and blessings be upon His noble Slave and Messenger, Muḥammad, Mercy to Mankind, and upon his family and all of his Companions.

Allāh Most High says, "Remember me and I will remember you" (Qur'ān 40:60) and "I have not created the Jinn or Humans but for My worship" (Qur'ān 51:56). We feel a sense of belonging, protection, and safety, when we call out to Allāh. And, when coupled with the powerful formulae of supplication and remembrance, this calling leads to a feeling of tranquility within our heart and mind. To facilitate this, Muslim scholars have compiled numerous books of supplications and remembrances from the Qur'ān and Prophetic Sunna. These works initially appeared in Arabic throughout the Muslim world for many centuries. Subsequently, many of these works have been translated into other languages.

In 1999, Allāh granted Shaykh Inam Uddin and myself the opportunity during our study at the Darul Uloom in Bury, UK, to compile a selection of prayers from existing Arabic sources for younger students to memorize. This endeavor eventually developed into a published work.

Before you is the third edition of this work, *Reflections of Pearls*, a short compilation of *duʿās* in Arabic, with English translations and transliterations along with sections on the virtues and excellences of various chapters and verses of the Qur'ān. Changes to the previous edition include: (1) the addition of several new *duʿās*, such as a new section on comprehensive *duʿās* from the Qur'ān; (2) improvements in language to enhance the fluency; (3) updates to a more academic and professional style of transliteration. The transliteration is one of the principal features of this work, which is why more emphasis has been drawn to it. However, we strongly recommend learning the *duʿās* from the Arabic text. The purpose of the transliteration is only to assist and guide the reader in this regard.

The Messenger of Allāh ﷺ said, "Whoever calls toward guidance, for him is the same reward as the one who follows him without their reward decreasing in anyway" (*Muslim*). This was our intention in the presentation of this work. Although there are many other books of *duʿās* available, this one has been well-received for its concise collection of important *duʿās*, and its presentation of those *duʿās* alongside the English transliteration and translation. Our primary concern has been to only include well-authenticated narrations, even though scholars overwhelmingly accept weak ḥadīth in non-legislative matters that pertain to excellences and virtues of worships (see *Tadrīb al-Rāwī* 2:488). Wherever a narration of a lesser degree of authenticity has been used we have tried to indicate it as such in the extended reference section at the back. A few *duʿās*, not from ḥadīth, but related from our pious predecessors, have also been included for their usefulness.

I am grateful to all of those who helped bring the third edition of this book to fruition, especially Farooq Ahmad for his persistence in the cover design and Osman Ali for continuously encouraging me to work on the book despite my other obligations, and for his help in compiling some of the new *duʿās* included in this edition.

May Allāh allow this work to inspire many seeking minds and grant solace to many yearning hearts! We ask from Allāh divine assistance and guidance, recourse to Him, protection from deviance, and success in our endeavors.

He is sufficient for us and He is the best Patron, and there is no power to do good or restraint to avoid evil except with Allāh.

Abdur-Rahman ibn Yusuf Mangera
Dhū 'l-Ḥijja 1425 | February 2005

Part 1

فضائل وآداب

Significance & Etiquette of Supplication

The Significance of Supplication

Duʿāʾ, "supplication" or "prayer," is the medium of direct communication between man and his Lord wherein man reveals his intimate feelings and desires: wherein he beseeches his Creator and Lord to fulfill his aspirations and needs.

Supplication is a refuge for those who have no place to go. It is a solace for the bereaved. It is a source of contentment and peace of mind at times of great distress. It is an inspiration for the hopeless. It is the expression of a man's loneliness, meekness, and inability in the court of Almighty Allāh. The significance and reality of *duʿāʾ* is explained in the following ḥadīth: Nuʿmān ibn Bashīr ﷺ relates that Allāh's Messenger ﷺ said, "*Duʿāʾ* is worship," then he recited the following verse: "And your Lord says 'Call on Me. I will answer you [i.e., your prayer]. Surely those who are too proud to serve Me will enter Hell abased'" (Qur'ān 40:60) (*Tirmidhī*). This ḥadīth has been explained to mean that *duʿāʾ* can be deemed a form of worship, as it embodies the very ethos of worship—firm attention toward Allāh.

This is substantiated by the narration of Anas ibn Mālik ﷺ in which the Messenger of Allāh ﷺ said, "*Duʿāʾ* is the essence of worship" (*Tirmidhī*) and the narration of Abū Hurayra ﷺ in which the Messenger of Allāh ﷺ said, "There is nothing as venerable in the sight of Allāh as *duʿāʾ*" (*Tirmidhī*). The Messenger of Allāh ﷺ is also reported to have said, "A person who does not invoke Allāh, Allāh becomes displeased with him" (*Tirmidhī*), and for him who desires that Allāh accept his *duʿās* in difficult times, it is necessary that he makes abundant *duʿāʾ* in good times" (*Tirmidhī*). "*Duʿāʾ* is a weapon of the believer, a pillar of the religion [Islam], and the light of the heavens and earth" (*Mustadrak*).

The Etiquette of Supplication

When supplicating to Allāh Most High, the following measures should be observed:

1. Abstain from unlawful (*ḥarām*) food, drink, and clothing.
2. Abstain from unlawful income.
3. Be sincere in what you ask for.
4. Attempt to perform a good deed before making the *duʿāʾ*.
5. Do not gaze toward the sky.
6. Confess one's sins.
7. Be in the state of purity in body and clothes.
8. Be in the state of *wuḍūʾ*.
9. Face the *qibla*.
10. Perform *Ṣalāt al-Ḥāja* (the prayer of need) before making *duʿāʾ*.
11. Adopt a sitting posture like that of prayer (*qaʿda*).
12. Praise Allāh before and after the *duʿāʾ*.
13. Send salutations and blessings upon the Messenger of Allāh ﷺ at the beginning and at the end of the *duʿāʾ*.
14. Raise both hands to chest level while making *duʿāʾ*.
15. Keep hands open and fingers slightly spread.
16. Bear in mind the greatness of Allāh Most High.
17. Plead to Allāh in utmost humility.
18. In times of difficulty, invoke Allāh through the mediation of any good deed one has performed.
19. Make *duʿāʾ* through the mediation of Allāh's beautiful names.
20. Make *duʿāʾ* through the mediation of the Prophets (upon them be peace).
21. Make *duʿāʾ* through the mediation of the pious servants of Allāh.
22. Abstain from deliberate singing and from affecting a rhythmic tone in the *duʿāʾ*.
23. Recite *duʿās* mentioned in various ḥadīths, for the Messenger of Allāh ﷺ did not leave out any aspect of human need for which he did not make *duʿāʾ*.
24. Begin by first making *duʿāʾ* for oneself, then for one's parents, then for the whole Umma.

25. The *imām* should include his congregation in his *duʿāʾ*.
26. Be realistic when making *duʿāʾ*. Do not ask Allāh for unreasonable things.
27. Say *āmīn* and encourage others to say *āmīn* after making *duʿāʾ*.
28. After completing the *duʿāʾ*, pass your hands over your face.
29. Do not set any conditions for Allāh such as: "O Allāh, if you wish to free me of my debts then free me." Instead, say: "O Allāh, free me of my debts."
30. Do not ask for anything that involves sin, for instance, the breaking of blood ties.
31. Do not be impatient, expecting the *duʿāʾ* to be granted immediately.
32. Make *duʿāʾ* with conviction regarding its acceptance.
33. The *duʿāʾ* should be made from the depth of the heart and with full concentration, for Allāh does not accept the *duʿāʾ* of a careless person.

Circumstances in Which Supplications are Accepted

1. While the call to prayer (*adhān*) is in progress.
2. The period between the *adhān* and the call to commence prayer (*iqāma*).
3. After the one making the call to prayer (*muʾadhdhin*) says *Ḥayya ʿalā ʾṣ-ṣalāh*, "come to prayer," and *Ḥayya ʿalā ʾl-falāḥ*, "come to success," especially for the person who is in pain and mourning.
4. When forming ranks in preparation for fighting in *jihād*.
5. When fighting in *jihād*, especially during its fiercest moments.
6. After the completion of obligatory (*farḍ*) prayers.
7. In the prostration (*sajda*) of prayer. However, this is to be restricted to non-obligatory prayers (according to the Ḥanafī school) and only those *duʿās* made which can only be asked of Allāh alone, like

forgiveness, Paradise, and so on—preferably those that appear in the Qur'ān and ḥadīths. It is excessively disliked (*makrūh taḥrīmī*) to make these *duʿās* in other than Arabic in the prayer.

8. After the recitation of a portion of the Holy Qur'ān.
9. After the completion of the Holy Qur'ān, either by the reciter or the listener.
10. While drinking the water of Zam Zam, especially at the well of Zam Zam.
11. When a person reaches his final breath in the world; either by the dying person himself or those around him.
12. When a cock crows.
13. When there is a gathering of many Muslims.
14. In a gathering wherein the remembrance of Allāh (*dhikr*) takes place, where the Holy Qur'ān is being taught or a religious lecture is being delivered.
15. When closing the eyelids of a dead person.
16. While the *mu'adhdhin* makes the call to commence (*iqāma*).
17. When it rains.
18. According to Imām Jazrī, *duʿā'* is certainly accepted (a) whenever a person sees the Kaʿba, (b) when the *duʿā'* is made between the two occasions where Allāh's name is mentioned in the following verse of Sūrat al-Anʿām:

وَإِذَا جَاءَتْهُمْ آيَةٌ قَالُوا لَن نُّؤْمِنَ حَتَّىٰ نُؤْتَىٰ مِثْلَ مَا أُوتِيَ رُسُلُ
اللَّهِ ۘ اللَّهُ أَعْلَمُ حَيْثُ يَجْعَلُ رِسَالَتَهُ ۗ . . .﴿١٢٤﴾

We will not believe until we are given [exactly] the like of what Allāh's Messengers were given. Allāh Knows best where to place His Message (Qur'ān 6:124).

Many scholars including Shaykh Imdād al-Maqdisī have confirmed the assured acceptance of *duʿā'* between the two words [Allāh and Allāh] in the above verse (*Al-Ḥiṣn al-Ḥaṣīn*).

Places Where Supplications are Accepted

Duʿās are accepted in all sacred places. For instance, they are accepted at the resting place of the Messenger of Allāh ﷺ. Imām Jazrī says: "If *duʿās* are not accepted at the blessed grave of the Messenger of Allāh ﷺ where else would they be accepted?" Ḥasan al-Baṣrī wrote a letter to the people of Makka wherein he listed all such places in Makka. Among them are the following:

1. The circuit (*maṭāf*) in which the circumambulation of the House of Allāh (Kaʿba) takes place.
2. The Multazam—the area between the Black Stone (al-Ḥajar al-Aswad) and the door of the Kaʿba.
3. Under the Water Spout (*Mīzāb*) of the Kaʿba.
4. Inside the Kaʿba.
5. At the well of Zam Zam.
6. On the Mounts of Ṣafā and Marwā.
7. In the area where pilgrims walk between Ṣafā and Marwā.
8. Behind the stone containing the footprint of Ibrāhīm عليه السلام (Maqām Ibrāhīm).
9. In the plain of ʿArafāt.
10. In Muzdalifa.
11. In Minā.
12. At the stone pillars (*jamarāt*) where the Satans are pelted.

People Whose Supplications are Accepted With Certainty

1. A destitute and helpless person.
2. An oppressed person, even if he is a non-believer or sinful.

3. Parent's *duʿāʾ* for their children.
4. The *duʿāʾ* of a just king or ruler.
5. The *duʿāʾ* of a righteous person.
6. *Duʿāʾ* of children who are kind and obedient to their parents.
7. *Duʿāʾ* of the wayfarer.
8. The *duʿāʾ* of a fasting person at the time of breaking the fast.
9. A Muslim's *duʿāʾ* for another in his or her absence.
10. Every *duʿāʾ* of a Muslim, so long as it is not for oppression or severing blood ties.
11. The pilgrim's *duʿāʾ* until he or she returns home.

Opportune Moments in Which Supplications are Accepted

1. On the night of *Qadr* (Destiny, Power—a blessed night in Ramaḍān when the angels descend to the world with peace).
2. On the day of ʿArafa.
3. During the month of Ramaḍān.
4. On the eve of Friday (the night preceding Friday).
5. During the entire day of Friday.
6. During the second half of the night.
7. During the first third portion of the night.
8. During the final third portion of the night.
9. During the middle of the final third portion of the night.
10. Prior to dawn (at time of *suḥūr*).
11. On Friday during the "Moment of Acceptance" (*sāʿat al-ijāba*). There is much difference of opinion amongst the scholars regarding this period. Some say it falls between the time when the *imām* gets up for the sermon and the completion of the Friday prayer. Others say it occurs while the Friday prayer is in progress. Some say its time is between the late afternoon prayer (ʿAṣr) and sunset while others say it is just moments before sunset. There are some

who say its time is from dawn till sunrise while others say its time is after sunrise. Abū Dharr al-Ghifārī ﷺ maintained that it falls just after zenith (*zawāl*) until the sun declines one arm's length. According to Imām Jazrī, the author of *Al-Ḥiṣn al-Ḥaṣīn,* its time occurs when the *imām* begins reciting Sūrat al-Fātiḥa to when he says *āmīn*. Perhaps the most acceptable opinion is that of Imām Nawawī—which is in agreement with the ḥadīth and hardly leaves room for conjecture—that its time is from when the imām sits on the pulpit until the end of the Friday prayer.

THE GREAT NAME OF ALLĀH (*ISM ALLĀH AL-Aʿẓam*)

ʿAbdullāh ibn Burayda relates from his father ﷺ that the Messenger of Allāh ﷺ heard someone say:

اَللّٰهُمَّ إِنِّيْ أَسْأَلُكَ بِأَنِّيْ أَشْهَدُ أَنَّكَ أَنْتَ اللّٰهُ لَا اِلٰهَ إِلَّا أَنْتَ الْأَحَدُ
الصَّمَدُ الَّذِيْ لَمْ يَلِدْ وَلَمْ يُوْلَدْ وَلَمْ يَكُنْ لَّهُ كُفُوًا أَحَدٌ

Allāhumma innī as'aluka bi annī ashhadu annaka Anta Allāhu lā ilāha illā Anta 'l-Aḥadu 'l-Ṣamadu 'lladhī lam yalid wa lam yūlad, wa lam yakul lahū kufuwan aḥad.

O Allāh, I ask of You as I bear witness that You are Allāh. There is none worthy of worship but You. You are unequaled, free from want. He does not beget nor is He begotten and none is equal unto Him.

So he ﷺ said, "He has asked Allāh using a name by which when asked Allāh gives and when called He answers" (*Abū Dāwūd, Nasā'ī, Tirmidhī, Ibn Māja, Aḥmad, Ibn Ḥibbān*).

Anas bin Mālik relates that he was sitting with the Messenger of Allāh ﷺ and a person was praying after which he began to make *duʿā'* and said:

اَللّٰهُمَّ إِنِّيْ أَسْأَلُكَ بِأَنَّ لَكَ الْحَمْدُ، لَا إِلٰهَ إِلَّا أَنْتَ الْمَنَّانُ بَدِيْعُ
السَّمٰوٰتِ وَالْأَرْضِ، يَا ذَا الْجَلَالِ وَالْإِكْرَامِ، يَا حَيُّ يَا قَيُّوْمُ ❁

Allāhumma innī as'aluka bi anna laka 'l-ḥamd(u), lā ilāha illā Anta 'l-Mannānu Badī-ᶜu 's-samāwāti wa 'l-arḍ(i), yā Dha 'l-jalāli wa 'l-ikrām(i), yā Ḥayyu yā Qayyūm.

O Allāh, I beg of You as all praise is to You alone. There is no god but You. You are Most Kind, Originator of the heavens and earth, O Lord of Majesty and Benevolence! O Ever Living Self-subsistent One!

So the Messenger of Allāh ﷺ said, "He called upon Allāh with His Great Name by which when He is called He answers, and when asked He gives (*Abū Dāwūd, Nasā'ī, Tirmidhī, Ibn Māja, Aḥmad*).

It is related from Asmā' bint Yazīd ﵂ that the Prophet ﷺ said, "The great name of Allāh is in the following two verses:

وَإِلَٰهُكُمْ إِلَٰهٌ وَاحِدٌ ۖ لَا إِلَٰهَ إِلَّا هُوَ الرَّحْمَٰنُ الرَّحِيمُ ﴿١٦٣﴾

Wa ilāhukum Ilāhuw Wāḥidul lā ilāha illā Huwa 'r-Raḥmānu 'r-Raḥīm.

And your God is one God. There is no god but He, the Compassionate, the Merciful (Qur'ān 2:163).

and the beginning verse of Sūra Āli ᶜImrān:

الٓمٓ ﴿١﴾ اللَّهُ لَا إِلَٰهَ إِلَّا هُوَ الْحَيُّ الْقَيُّومُ ﴿٢﴾

Alif Lām Mīm, Allāhu lā ilāha illā Huwa 'l-Ḥayyu 'l-Qayyūm.

Alif Lām Mīm! Allāh is He besides Whom there is no god—the Everlasting, the Self-Subsistent" (Qur'ān 3:1–2) (*Tirmidhī*).

It is related from Saʿd ibn Abī Waqqās ﷺ that the Messenger of Allāh ﷺ said, "The call of Dhū 'l-Nūn, when he called, while in the belly of the whale:

لَا إِلَٰهَ إِلَّا أَنْتَ سُبْحَانَكَ إِنِّي كُنْتُ مِنَ الظَّالِمِينَ ﴿٨٧﴾

Lā ilāha illā Anta subḥānaka innī kuntu mina 'ẓ-ẓālimīn.

There is no god but You. Exalted are You. I am indeed of the transgressors (Qur'ān 21:87).

No Muslim ever calls upon Allāh by it regarding anything except that Allāh answers him" (*Tirmidhī*).

Part 2

الأدعية اليومية

Everyday Supplications

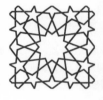

1. AT THE TIME OF SLEEPING

اَللّٰهُمَّ بِاسْمِكَ أَمُوْتُ وَأَحْيٰ ۞

Allāhumma bi 'smika amūtu wa aḥyā.

O Allāh, by Your name I die and live (*Bukhārī*).[1]

اَللّٰهُمَّ أَسْلَمْتُ نَفْسِيْ إِلَيْكَ، وَوَجَّهْتُ وَجْهِيْ إِلَيْكَ، وَفَوَّضْتُ أَمْرِيْ إِلَيْكَ، وَأَلْجَأْتُ ظَهْرِيْ إِلَيْكَ رَغْبَةً وَّرَهْبَةً إِلَيْكَ، لَا مَلْجَأَ وَلَا مَنْجٰى مِنْكَ إِلَّا إِلَيْكَ، آمَنْتُ بِكِتَابِكَ الَّذِيْ أَنْزَلْتَ وَنَبِيِّكَ الَّذِيْ أَرْسَلْتَ ۞

Allāhumma aslamtu nafsī ilayk(a), wa wajjahtu wajhī ilayk(a), wa fawwattu amrī ilayk(a), wa alja'tu ẓahrī ilayka raghbataw wa rahbatan ilayk(a), lā malja'a wa lā manjā minka illā ilayk(a). Āmantu bi kitābika 'lladhī anzalta wa nabiyyika 'lladhī arsalt.

O Allāh, I have surrendered my life to You and turned my face toward You and entrusted all my affairs to You and wholly placed my reliance in You. [All this I do] to gain Your mercy and due to fear of Your punishment. There is no protection from Your wrath except through Your mercy. I believe in the Book You have revealed and in the Prophet You have sent.

Whoever recites this *duʿā'*, then passes away in the night, will be counted as having passed away on Islam. If he wakes up in the morning, he will wake up on goodness (*Bukhārī, Muslim*).[2]

2. WHEN WAKING-UP

اَلْحَمْدُ لِلّٰهِ الَّذِيْ أَحْيَانَا بَعْدَ مَا أَمَاتَنَا وَإِلَيْهِ النُّشُوْرُ ❁

Al-ḥamdu li 'Llāhi 'lladhī aḥyānā baʿda
mā amātanā wa ilayhi 'n-nushūr.

Praise be to Allāh who gave us life after having given us death, and to Him is [our] final return (*Bukhārī, Muslim*).[3]

3. BEFORE ENTERING THE LAVATORY

بِسْمِ اللّٰهِ، اَللّٰهُمَّ إِنِّيْ أَعُوْذُ بِكَ مِنَ الْخُبُثِ وَالْخَبَائِثِ ❁

Bismi 'Llāh(i), Allāhumma innī a-ʿūdhū bika
mina 'l-khubuthi wa 'l-khabā'ith.

In the name of Allāh:[4] O Allāh, I seek Your protection from male and female demons (*Bukhārī, Muslim*).[5]

4. AFTER LEAVING THE LAVATORY

غُفْرَانَكَ، الْحَمْدُ لِلّٰهِ الَّذِيْ أَذْهَبَ عَنِّي الْأَذٰى وَعَافَانِيْ ❁

Ghufrānak(a), (a)l-ḥamdu li 'Llāhi 'lladhī
adhhaba ʿannī 'l-adhā wa ʿāfānī.

[O Allāh,] I seek Your forgiveness. Praise be to Allāh who relieved me of discomfort and granted me comfort (*Abū Dāwūd, Tirmidhī*).[6]

5. BEFORE BEGINNING ABLUTION (*WUḌŪ'*)

اَللّٰهُمَّ اغْفِرْ لِيْ ذَنْبِيْ، وَوَسِّعْ لِيْ فِيْ دَارِيْ، وَبَارِكْ لِيْ فِيْ رِزْقِيْ ❁

Allāhumma ʼghfir lī dhambī, wa wassiʿ
lī fī dārī, wa bārik lī fī rizqī.

O Allāh, forgive me my sin, make spacious my home
and blessed my sustenance (Ibn al-Sunnī).[7]

6. AT THE END OF ABLUTION (*WUḌŪʼ*)

أَشْهَدُ أَن لَّا إِلٰهَ إِلَّا اللّٰهُ وَحْدَهُ لَا شَرِيْكَ لَهُ
وَأَشْهَدُ أَنَّ مُحَمَّدًا عَبْدُهُ وَرَسُوْلُهُ ۞

Ashhadu al lā ilāha illa ʼLlāhu waḥdahū lā sharīka lahū wa ashhadu anna Muḥammadan ʿabduhū wa rasūluh.

I bear witness that there is no god but Allāh. He
is one and has no partner and I bear witness that
Muḥammad is His Servant and Messenger.

Whoever recites this *duʿā*ʼ, the eight doors of Paradise will be opened for him (*Muslim*).[8]

Then recite the following:

اَللّٰهُمَّ اجْعَلْنِي مِنَ التَّوَّابِيْنَ وَاجْعَلْنِي مِنَ الْمُتَطَهِّرِيْنَ ۞

Allāhumma ʼj-ʿalnī mina ʼt-tawwābīna wa
ʼj-ʿalnī mina ʼl-mutaṭahhirīn.

O Allāh, make me of those who repent and of those
who maintain purity (*Nasāʼī, Tirmidhī*).[9]

7. AFTER HEARING THE CALL TO PRAYER (*ADHĀN*)

First send blessings and salutations (*ṣalawāt*) upon the Messenger of Allāh ﷺ (*Muslim*), then recite the following:

اَللّٰهُمَّ رَبَّ هٰذِهِ الدَّعْوَةِ التَّامَّةِ وَالصَّلَاةِ الْقَائِمَةِ، آتِ مُحَمَّدَنِ
الْوَسِيْلَةَ وَالْفَضِيْلَةَ، وَابْعَثْهُ مَقَامًا مَّحْمُوْدَنِ الَّذِيْ وَعَدتَّهُ ۞

Allāhumma Rabba hādhihi 'd-daʿwati 't-tāmmati wa 'ṣ-ṣalāt 'il-qā'ima(ti), āti Muḥammadani 'l-wasīlata wa 'l-faḍīla(ta), wa 'bʿathhu maqāmam maḥmūdani 'lladhī wa ʿattah.

O Allāh, Lord of this perfect call and established prayer, grant Muḥammad a place near to You, an excellence and exalted degree, and raise him to the praiseworthy station that You have promised him.

Whoever recites this *duʿā'* will gain the intercession of the Messenger of Allāh ﷺ on the Day of Judgment (*Bukhārī*).[10]

8. WHEN ENTERING THE *MASJID*

اَللّٰهُمَّ افْتَحْ لِيْ أَبْوَابَ رَحْمَتِكَ ۞

Allāhumma 'ftaḥ lī abwāba raḥmatik.

O Allāh, open for me the doors of Your mercy.

Before reciting this *duʿā',* one should send blessings and salutations (*ṣalawāt*) upon the Messenger of Allāh ﷺ (*Muslim*).[11]

9. WHEN LEAVING THE *MASJID*

اَللّٰهُمَّ إِنِّيْ أَسْأَلُكَ مِنْ فَضْلِكَ ۞

Allāhumma innī as'aluka min faḍlik.

O Allāh, I ask of You Your favor (*Muslim*).[12]

10. BEFORE EATING

بِسْمِ اللّٰهِ وَبَرَكَةِ اللّٰهِ ❁

Bismi 'Llāhi wa barakati 'Llāh.

In the name of Allāh and with the blessings of Allāh (*Mustadrak*).[13]

11. AFTER EATING

اَلْحَمْدُ لِلّٰهِ الَّذِيْ أَطْعَمَنَا وَسَقَانَا وَجَعَلَنَا مُسْلِمِيْنَ ❁

Al-ḥamdu li 'Llāhi 'lladhī aṭʿamanā wa saqānā wa ja-ʿalanā muslimīn.

Praise be to Allāh who fed us and gave us to drink and made us Muslims (*Abū Dāwūd, Tirmidhī*).[14]

~

اَلْحَمْدُ لِلّٰهِ الَّذِيْ أَطْعَمَنِيْ هٰذَا الطَّعَامَ،
وَرَزَقَنِيْهِ مِنْ غَيْرِ حَوْلٍ مِّنِّيْ وَلَا قُوَّةٍ ❁

Al-ḥamdu li 'Llāhi 'lladhī aṭʿamanī hādha 't-ṭa-ʿām(a), wa raza-qanīhi min ghayri ḥawlim minnī wa lā qūwwah.

Praise be to Allāh who fed me this food and bestowed it upon me without any strength and ability on my part.

Whoever recites this *duʿā'*, his past sins are forgiven (*Abū Dāwūd, Tirmidhī*).[15]

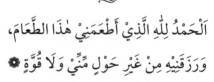

12. IF ONE FORGETS THE SUPPLICATION BEFORE EATING, THEN UPON REMEMBERING ONE SHOULD RECITE

بِسْمِ اللّٰهِ اَوَّلَهٗ وَأٰخِرَهٗ ❁

Bismi 'Llāhi awwalahū wa ākhirahū.

In the name of Allāh, at the beginning of it [the meal] and at the end of it (*Abū Dāwūd*).[16]

13. AT THE TIME OF COMPLETING THE FAST

اَللّٰهُمَّ إِنِّيْ أَسْأَلُكَ بِرَحْمَتِكَ الَّتِيْ وَسِعَتْ كُلَّ شَيْءٍ أَنْ تَغْفِرَ لِيْ ❁

Allāhumma innī as'aluka bi raḥmatika 'llatī wasi-ʿat kulla shay'in an taghfira lī.

O Allāh, Verily I ask You, by Your mercy which encompasses everything, to forgive me (*Ibn Māja*).[17]

~

اَللّٰهُمَّ لَكَ صُمْتُ وَعَلٰى رِزْقِكَ أَفْطَرْتُ ❁

Allāhumma laka ṣumtu wa ʿalā rizqika afṭart.

O Allāh, for You have I fasted, and by what [food] You have blessed me with have I broken it (Abū Dāwūd in his *Marāsīl*).[18]

14. WHEN DINING AT SOMEONE'S HOUSE OR AFTER PARTAKING FOOD BY INVITATION

اَللّٰهُمَّ أَطْعِمْ مَنْ أَطْعَمَنِيْ وَاسْقِ مَنْ سَقَانِيْ ❁

Allāhumma aṭᶜim man aṭᶜamanī wa ʼsqi man saqānī.

O Allāh, feed those who have fed me and sate those who have sated me (*Muslim*).[19]

15. AFTER DRINKING MILK

اَللّٰهُمَّ بَارِكْ لَنَا فِيْهِ وَزِدْنَا مِنْهُ ۞

Allāhumma bārik lanā fīhi wa zidnā minh.

O Allāh, bless us by it, and increase us in it (*Tirmidhī*).[20]

16. WHEN DRINKING THE WATER OF ZAM ZAM

اَللّٰهُمَّ إِنِّيْ أَسْأَلُكَ عِلْمًا نَّافِعًا، وَّرِزْقًا وَّاسِعًا، وَّشِفَاءً مِّنْ كُلِّ دَاءٍ ۞

Allāhumma innī as'aluka ᶜilman nāfi-ᶜaw wa rizqaw wāsi-ᶜaw wa shifā'am min kulli dā'.

O Allāh, I ask of You, beneficial knowledge, ample provisions, and restoration from every illness (*Mustadrak*).[21]

17. WHEN PUTTING ON AN ARTICLE OF CLOTHING

اَلْحَمْدُ لِلّٰهِ الَّذِيْ كَسَانِيْ هٰذَا الثَّوْبَ، وَرَزَقَنِيْهِ
مِنْ غَيْرِ حَوْلٍ مِّنِّيْ وَلَا قُوَّةٍ ۞

Al-ḥamdu li ʼLlāhi ʼlladhī kasānī hādha ʼth-thawb(a), wa razaqanīhi min ghayri ḥawlim minnī wa lā quwwah.

Praise be to Allāh who clothed me in this garment and gave it to me without any strength and ability on my part.

Whoever recites this *duʿā'*, his past and present sins will be forgiven (*Abū Dāwūd, Tirmidhī*).[22]

18. WHEN WEARING NEW CLOTHING

اَلْحَمْدُ لِلّٰهِ الَّذِيْ كَسَانِيْ مَا أُوَارِيْ بِهٖ
عَوْرَتِيْ، وَأَتَجَمَّلُ بِهٖ فِيْ حَيَاتِيْ ۞

Al-ḥamdu li 'Llāhi 'lladhī kasānī mā uwārī bihī ʿawratī, wa atajammalu bihī fī ḥayātī.

Praise be to Allāh who clothed me with what covers my nakedness, and with that by which I adorn myself in my life (*Tirmidhī*).[23]

19. BEFORE REMOVING CLOTHING AT THE TIME OF SLEEPING, CHANGING, ETC.

بِسْمِ اللّٰهِ الَّذِيْ لَا إِلٰهَ إِلَّا هُوَ ۞

Bismi 'Llāhi 'lladhī lā ilāha illā hū.

In the name of Allāh besides whom there is no god (Ibn al-Sunnī).[24]

20. WHEN OBSERVING SOMEONE WEARING NEW CLOTHES

اِلْبَسْ جَدِيْدًا، وَّعِشْ حَمِيْدًا، وَّمُتْ شَهِيْدًا ۞

Ilbas jadīdan[w], wa ʿish ḥamīdān[w], wa mut shahīdā.

May you wear new clothing, live well, and die a martyr (*Ibn Māja*).[25]

21. WHILE LEAVING THE HOME

بِسْمِ اللّٰهِ تَوَكَّلْتُ عَلَى اللّٰهِ، اَللّٰهُمَّ إِنِّيْ أَعُوْذُ بِكَ أَنْ أُضِلَّ أَوْ أُضَلَّ، أَوْ أُزِلَّ أَوْ أُزَلَّ، أَوْ أَظْلِمَ أَوْ أُظْلَمَ، أَوْ أَجْهَلَ أَوْ يُجْهَلَ عَلَيَّ ❁

Bismi 'Llāhi tawakkaltu ʿala 'Llāh(i), Allāhumma innī a-ʿūdhu bika an uḍilla aw uḍall(a), aw uzilla aw uzall(a), aw aẓlima aw uẓlam(a), aw aj-hala aw yuj-hala ʿalayy.

In the name of Allāh, I trust in Allāh. O Allāh I seek your protection from misleading and being mislead, from causing someone to slip or slipping, from oppressing and oppression, and from promoting folly and being foolish (*Abū Dāwūd, Tirmidhī*).[26]

~

بِسْمِ اللّٰهِ تَوَكَّلْتُ عَلَى اللّٰهِ، وَلَا حَوْلَ وَلَا قُوَّةَ إِلَّا بِاللّٰهِ ❁

Bismi 'Llāhi tawakkaltu ʿala 'Llāh(i), wa lā ḥawla wa lā quwwata illā bi 'Llāh.

In the name of Allāh, I depend on Allāh, and there is no power [to do good] or restraint [to avoid evil] except with Allāh.

When anyone reads this *duʿā'*, the Angels say to him "You have been guided aright and have been saved [from all harms]" (*Abū Dāwūd, Tirmidhī*).[27]

22. WHILE ENTERING THE HOME

اَللّٰهُمَّ إِنِّيْ أَسْأَلُكَ خَيْرَ الْمَوْلِجِ وَخَيْرَ الْمَخْرَجِ، بِسْمِ اللّٰهِ وَلَجْنَا وَبِسْمِ اللّٰهِ خَرَجْنَا، وَعَلَى اللّٰهِ رَبِّنَا تَوَكَّلْنَا ❁

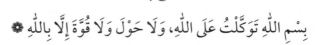

Allāhumma innī as'aluka khayra 'l-mawliji wa khayra 'l-makhraj(i), bismi 'Llāhi walajnā wa bismi 'Llāhi kharajnā, wa ʿala 'Llāhi Rabbinā tawakkalnā.

O Allāh, I beg of You the blessing of entering and leaving. In Allāh's name we enter and in Allāh's name we leave, and in Allāh, our Lord, we trust (*Abū Dāwūd*).[28]

23. WHEN LOOKING IN THE MIRROR

اَلْحَمْدُ لِلّٰهِ، اَللّٰهُمَّ كَمَا حَسَّنْتَ خَلْقِي فَحَسِّنْ خُلُقِي ۞

Al-ḥamdu li 'Llāh(i), Allāhumma kamā
ḥassanta khalqī fa ḥassin khuluqī.

Praise be to Allāh, O Allāh, as you have given me a good physical form, so favor me with good character (Ibn al-Sunnī).[29]

24. PRAYERS FOR THE MORNING AND EVENING

بِسْمِ اللّٰهِ الَّذِيْ لَا يَضُرُّ مَعَ اسْمِهٖ شَيْءٌ فِي الْأَرْضِ
وَلَا فِي السَّمَاءِ وَهُوَ السَّمِيْعُ الْعَلِيْمُ ۞

Bismi 'Llāhi 'lladhī lā yaḍurru ma-ʿa 'smihī shay'un fi
'l-arḍi wa lā fi 's-samā'i wa Huwa 's-Samī-ʿul ʿAlīm.

In the name of Allāh by whose name nothing
on earth and nothing in heaven can cause
harm. He is All-Hearing, All-Knowing.

Whoever reads this *duʿā'* thrice in the morning or evening, nothing will harm him till the night or morning (*Muslim, Abū Dāwūd, Tirmidhī*).[30]

رَضِيْنَا بِاللّٰهِ رَبًّا، وَّبِالْإِسْلَامِ دِيْنًا، وَّبِمُحَمَّدٍ رَّسُوْلًا ❁

Raḍīnā bi 'Llāhi rabbaw wa bi 'l-Islāmi
dīnaw wa bi Muḥammadin rasūlā.

We are pleased with Allāh as the Lord, with Islam as
the Religion and with Muḥammad as the Messenger.

Whoever recites this *duʿā'* in the morning, Allāh will satisfy him and please him (*Abū Dāwūd*).[31]

25. WHEN BIDDING FAREWELL TO SOMEONE

أَسْتَوْدِعُ اللّٰهَ دِيْنَكَ وَأَمَانَتَكَ وَخَوَاتِيْمَ عَمَلِكَ ❁

Astawdi-ʿu 'Llāha dīnaka wa amānataka
wa khawātīma ʿamalik.

I entrust Allāh with your religion, your belongings
and the result of your deeds (*Tirmidhī*).[32]

26. WHEN BOARDING A VEHICLE OR MOUNTING AN ANIMAL

While boarding or mounting recite first:

بِسْمِ اللّٰهِ ❁

Bismi 'Llāh, In the name of Allāh.

When comfortably seated and ready to go, recite:

اَلْحَمْدُ لِلّٰهِ ❁

Al-ḥamdu li 'Llāh, Praise be to Allāh.

Then recite:

سُبْحَانَ الَّذِيْ سَخَّرَ لَنَا هٰـذَا وَمَا كُنَّا لَهُ مُقْرِنِيْنَ ﴿١٣﴾

وَإِنَّا إِلَى رَبِّنَا لَمُنْقَلِبُوْنَ ﴿١٤﴾

Subḥāna 'lladhī sakhkhara lanā hādhā wa mā kunnā lahū muqrinīn(a). Wa innā ilā Rabbinā la munqalibūn.

Exalted is He who subjected this to us, and we could not have subdued it: verily to our Lord we return (Qur'ān 43:13).

Thereafter, recite thrice:

اَلْحَمْدُ لِلّٰهِ

Al-ḥamdu li 'Llāh, Praise be to Allāh.

Then thrice:

اَللّٰهُ أَكْبَرُ

Allāhu Akbar, Allāh is the Greatest.

Thereafter recite the following prayer for forgiveness (*istighfār*):

سُبْحَانَكَ إِنِّيْ ظَلَمْتُ نَفْسِيْ فَاغْفِرْ لِيْ،

إِنَّهُ لَا يَغْفِرُ الذُّنُوْبَ إِلَّا أَنْتَ

Subḥānaka innī ẓalamtu nafsī fa 'ghfir lī,
innahū lā yaghfiru 'dh-dhunūba illā Ant.

Exalted are You (O Allāh). Verily, I have wronged myself so forgive me as none but You forgives sins (*Abū Dāwūd, Tirmidhī*).[33]

Also recite:

اَللّٰهُمَّ إِنِّيْ أَسْأَلُكَ فِيْ سَفَرِيْ هٰذَا مِنَ الْبِرِّ وَالتَّقْوٰى وَمِنَ الْعَمَلِ مَا تَرْضٰى. اَللّٰهُمَّ هَوِّنْ عَلَيْنَا الْمَسِيْرَ وَاطْوِ عَنَّا بُعْدَ الْأَرْضِ. اَللّٰهُمَّ أَنْتَ الصَّاحِبُ فِي السَّفَرِ وَالْخَلِيْفَةُ فِي الْأَهْلِ. اَللّٰهُمَّ أَصْحِبْنَا فِي السَّفَرِ وَاخْلُفْنَا فِيْ أَهْلِنَا. اَللّٰهُمَّ إِنِّيْ أَعُوْذُ بِكَ مِنْ وَعْثَاءِ السَّفَرِ، وَكَاٰبَةِ الْمُنْقَلَبِ، وَمِنَ الْحَوْرِ بَعْدَ الْكَوْرِ، وَمِنْ دَعْوَةِ الْمَظْلُوْمِ، وَسُوْءِ الْمَنْظَرِ فِي الْأَهْلِ وَالْمَالِ ❁

Allāhumma innī as'aluka fī safarī hādhā mina 'l-birri wa 't-taqwā wa mina 'l-ʿamali mā tarḍā. Allāhumma hawwin ʿalaynā 'l-masīra wa 'ṭwi ʿannā buʿda 'l-arḍ(i). Allāhumma Anta 'ṣ-ṣāḥibu fī 's-safari wa 'l-khalīfatu fī 'l-ahl(i). Allāhumma aṣḥibnā fī 's-safari wa 'khlufnā fī ahlinā. Allāhumma innī a-ʿūdhu bika min waʿthā'i 's-safar(i), wa ka'ābati 'l-munqalab(i), wa mina 'l-ḥawri baʿda 'l-kawr(i), wa min daʿwati 'l-maẓlūm(i), wa sū'i 'l-manẓari fī 'l-ahli wa 'l-māl.

O Allāh, on this my journey I ask of You virtue, piety and actions that please You. O Allāh, make easy for us the passage and fold up for us the earth's expanse. O Allāh, You are the companion in travel, and the guardian of the family. O Allāh, accompany us in travel, and guard our family. O Allāh, I seek refuge in You from the hardships of travel, and from an ill return, from decrease after increase, from the supplications of the oppressed, and from an evil circumstance befalling my family and wealth (*Tirmidhī*).[34]

27. WHEN RETURNING HOME FROM A JOURNEY

آيِبُوْنَ تَائِبُوْنَ عَابِدُوْنَ لِرَبِّنَا حَامِدُوْنَ ۞

Ā'ibūna tā'ibūna ʿābidūna li Rabbinā ḥāmidūn.

We now return [from our journey] repenting [to Allāh], worshipping [Him], and praising our Lord [Allāh] (*Bukhārī*).[35]

28. AT THE TERMINATION OF A GATHERING (OF SACRED KNOWLEDGE OR RELIGIOUS DISCUSSION)

سُبْحَانَكَ اللّٰهُمَّ وَبِحَمْدِكَ، أَشْهَدُ أَن لَّا إِلٰهَ

إِلَّا أَنْتَ، أَسْتَغْفِرُكَ وَأَتُوْبُ إِلَيْكَ ۞

Subḥānaka 'Llāhumma wa bi ḥamdika, ashhadu al lā ilāha illā Ant(a), astaghfiruka wa atūbu ilayk.

Exalted are You, O Allāh, by Your praise: I bear witness that there is no god but You. I seek forgiveness from You and I repent to You.

Whoever recites this *duʿā'* will have all the sins committed by him in the gathering forgiven (*Tirmidhī, Mustadrak*).[36]

29. WHEN SNEEZING

اَلْحَمْدُ لِلّٰهِ ۞

Al-ḥamdu li 'Llāh, Praise be to Allāh.

One who hears it should respond by saying:

يَرْحَمُكَ اللّٰهُ ۞

Yarḥamuka ʼLlāh, Allāh's mercy be upon you.

Then the one who sneezed, upon hearing the response, should say:

يَهْدِيْكُمُ اللّٰهُ وَيُصْلِحُ بَالَكُمْ ۞

Yahdīkumu ʼLlāhu wa yuṣliḥu bālakum.

May Allāh guide you and rectify your condition (*Bukhārī*).[37]

30. WHEN THANKING SOMEBODY

جَزَاكَ اللّٰهُ خَيْرًا ۞

Jazāka ʼLlāhu khayran.

May Allāh reward you well (*Tirmidhī*).[38]

A person should say this to Muslims instead of "Thank You."

31. WHEN SEEING A MUSLIM HAPPY

أَضْحَكَ اللّٰهُ سِنَّكَ ۞

Aḍḥaka ʼLlāhu sinnak.

May Allāh fill your life with laughter (*Bukhārī, Abū Dāwūd*).[39]

32. WHEN ENTERING A MARKET OR SHOPPING CENTER

لَا إِلٰهَ إِلَّا اللّٰهُ وَحْدَهُ لَا شَرِيْكَ لَهُ، لَهُ الْمُلْكُ وَلَهُ

الْحَمْدُ، يُحْيِي وَيُمِيتُ، وَهُوَ حَيٌّ لَّا يَمُوتُ،

بِيَدِهِ الْخَيْرُ، وَهُوَ عَلَىٰ كُلِّ شَيْءٍ قَدِيرٌ ۞

Lā ilāha illa 'Llāhu waḥdahū lā sharīka lah(ū),
lahu 'l-mulku wa lahu 'l-ḥamd(u), yuḥyī wa
yumīt(u), wa Huwa Ḥayyul lā yamūt(u), bi yadihi
'l-khayr(u), wa Huwa ʿalā kulli shay'in qadīr.

There is no god but Allāh. He is One and has no partner. His is the Kingdom and to Him is all praise. He gives life and gives death. He is living, not subject to death. In His hand is goodness and He has power over all things.

Whoever recites this *duʿā'*, Allāh will award him a million good deeds, forgive a million of his sins, and raise his rank by a million degrees (*Tirmidhī, Mustadrak*).[40]

~

بِاسْمِ اللّٰهِ، اَللّٰهُمَّ إِنِّيْ أَسْأَلُكَ خَيْرَ هٰذِهِ السُّوْقِ وَخَيْرَ مَا فِيْهَا،

وَأَعُوْذُ بِكَ مِنْ شَرِّهَا وَشَرِّ مَا فِيْهَا. اَللّٰهُمَّ إِنِّيْ أَعُوْذُ بِكَ أَنْ

أُصِيْبَ فِيْهَا يَمِيْنًا فَاجِرَةً أَوْ صَفْقَةً خَاسِرَةً ۞

Bismi 'Llāhi Allāhumma innī as'aluka khayra hādhihi 's-sūqi
wa khayra mā fīhā, wa aʿūdhu bika min sharrihā wa sharri
mā fīhā. Allāhumma innī a-ʿūdhu bika an uṣība fīhā yamīnan
fājiratan aw ṣafqatan khāsirah.

In the name of Allāh. O Allāh, I beg of You the good of this market and what it contains, and I seek Your protection from the evil of this market and what it contains. O Allāh, I seek

Your protection from indulging in a false oath or becoming involved in a poor deal (*Mustadrak*).[41]

33. WHEN SEEING A FIRE

اَللّٰهُ أَكْبَرُ ۞

Allāhu Akbar, Allāh is the Greatest (Ibn al-Sunnī).[42]

34. WHEN HEARING THE BARKING OF A DOG OR BRAYING OF A DONKEY

أَعُوْذُ بِاللّٰهِ مِنَ الشَّيْطَانِ الرَّجِيْمِ ۞

A-ʿūdhu bi 'Llāhi mina 'sh-shayṭāni 'r-rajīm.

I seek refuge in Allāh from Satan, the accursed (*Abū Dāwūd*).[43]

35. WHEN BECOMING FRUSTRATED ABOUT PAYING A DEBT

اَللّٰهُمَّ اكْفِنِيْ بِحَلَالِكَ عَنْ حَرَامِكَ،
وَأَغْنِنِيْ بِفَضْلِكَ عَمَّنْ سِوَاكَ ۞

Allāhumma 'kfinī bi ḥalālika ʿan ḥarāmik(a),
wa aghninī bi faḍlika ʿamman siwāk.

O Allāh, suffice me with what You have made lawful in place of what You have made unlawful, and by Your grace free me of the need for anyone besides You.

Whoever recites this *duʿā'*, Allāh will assist him in repaying his debt even though it be the size of Mount Ṣīr [or Ṣabīr in Yemen] (*Tirmidhī*).[44]

36. WHEN AFRAID OF A GROUP OR NATION

اَللّٰهُمَّ إِنَّا نَجْعَلُكَ فِيْ نُحُوْرِهِمْ، وَنَعُوْذُ بِكَ مِنْ شُرُوْرِهِمْ ۞

Allāhumma innā najʿaluka fī nuḥūrihim,
wa na-ʿūdhu bika min shurūrihim.

O Allāh, we place You before them and seek You protection against their evil (*Abū Dāwūd*).[45]

37. WHEN FEELING PAIN IN THE BODY

أَعُوْذُ بِعِزَّةِ اللّٰهِ وَقُدْرَتِهٖ مِنْ شَرِّ مَا أَجِدُ وَأُحَاذِرُ ۞

A-ʿūdhu bi ʿizzati 'Llāhi wa qudratihī
min sharri mā ajidu wa uḥādhir.

I seek refuge in the might and power of Allāh,
from the evil of the pain I feel and fear.

Place the right hand on the affected area and recite *Bismi 'Llāh* thrice, thereafter recite the above-mentioned *duʿā'* seven times (*Muslim*).[46]

38. WHEN FEELING HELPLESS REGARDING A MATTER

حَسْبِيَ اللّٰهُ وَنِعْمَ الْوَكِيْلُ ۞

Ḥasbiya 'Llāhu wa niʿma 'l-wakīl.

Allāh is my sufficiency, and how perfect a benefactor [is He] (*Abū Dāwūd*).[47]

39. WHEN FACED WITH GRIEF OR SORROW

لَا إِلٰهَ إِلَّا اللّٰهُ الْعَظِيْمُ الْحَلِيْمُ، لَا إِلٰهَ إِلَّا اللّٰهُ رَبُّ الْعَرْشِ الْعَظِيْمِ، لَا إِلٰهَ إِلَّا اللّٰهُ رَبُّ السَّمَاوَاتِ وَرَبُّ الْأَرْضِ رَبُّ الْعَرْشِ الْكَرِيْمِ ۞

Lā ilāha illa 'Llāhu 'l-ʿAẓīmu 'l-Ḥalīm(u), Lā ilāha illa 'Llāhu Rabbu 'l-ʿarshi 'l-ʿaẓīm(i), Lā ilāha illa 'Llāhu Rabbu 's-samā-wāti wa Rabbu 'l-arḍi wa Rabbu 'l-ʿarshi 'l-karīm.

There is no god but Allāh, the August, the Enduring. There is no god but Allāh, the Lord of the Great Throne. There is no god but Allāh, the Lord of the Heavens and Earth and the Lord of the Throne of Honor (*Bukhārī, Muslim*).[48]

~

يَا حَيُّ يا قَيُّوْمُ، بِرَحْمَتِكَ أَسْتَغِيْثُ ۞

Yā Ḥayyu yā Qayyūm(u), bi raḥmatika astaghīth.

O You, the Everlasting and All-Sustainer, persistently do I invoke Your mercy (*Mustadrak*).[49]

~

لَا إِلَـٰهَ إِلَّا أَنْتَ سُبْحَانَكَ إِنِّي كُنْتُ مِنَ الظَّالِمِيْنَ ﴿٨٧﴾

Lā ilāha illā Anta subḥānaka innī kuntu mina 'ẓ-ẓālimīn.

There is no god but You, Exalted are You, I was of the transgressors (Qur'ān 21:87) (Ibn al-Sunnī).

40. WHEN SEEING SOMEONE IN DIFFICULTY

اَلْحَمْدُ لِلّٰهِ الَّذِيْ عَافَانِيْ مِمَّا ابْتَلَاكَ بِهٖ، وَفَضَّلَنِيْ
عَلٰى كَثِيْرٍ مِّمَّنْ خَلَقَ تَفْضِيْلًا ۞

Al-ḥamdu li 'Llāhi 'lladhī ʿāfānī mimma 'btalāka bih(ī),
wa faḍḍalanī ʿalā kathīrim mimman khalaqa tafḍillā.

Praise be to Allāh who has granted me safety from
the difficulty you are in and has favored me over
a great part of His creation (*Tirmidhī*).[50]

This *duʿā'* should be read in a low voice so the person in difficulty does not hear.

41. WHEN SOMETHING BAD OCCURS

اَلْحَمْدُ لِلّٰهِ عَلٰى كُلِّ حَالٍ ۞

Al-ḥamdu li 'Llāhi ʿalā kulli ḥāl.

Praise be to Allāh, in every state (*Mustadrak*).[51]

42. WHEN SOMETHING PLEASING OCCURS

اَلْحَمْدُ لِلّٰهِ الَّذِيْ بِنِعْمَتِهٖ تَتِمُّ الصَّالِحَاتُ ۞

Al-ḥamdu li 'Llāhi 'lladhī bi niʿmatihī tatimmu 'ṣ-ṣāliḥāt.

Praise be to Allāh, by whose grace all good
things are perfected (*Mustadrak*).[52]

43. WHEN ONE BECOMES ANGRY

أَعُوْذُ بِاللّٰهِ مِنَ الشَّيْطَانِ الرَّجِيْمِ ❁

A-ʿūdhu bi 'Llāhi mina 'sh-shayṭāni 'r-rajīm.

I seek refuge in Allāh from Satan, the accursed (*Bukhārī, Muslim*).[53]

44. WHEN UNABLE TO SLEEP AT NIGHT

اَللّٰهُمَّ غَارَتِ النُّجُوْمُ، وَهَدَأَتِ الْعُيُوْنُ، وَأَنْتَ حَيٌّ قَيُّوْمٌ، لَّا تَأْخُذُكَ سِنَةٌ وَّلَا نَوْمٌ، يَّا حَيُّ يَا قَيُّوْمُ، أَهْدِأْ لَيْلِيْ وَأَنِمْ عَيْنِيْ ❁

Allāhumma ghārati 'n-nujūm(u), wa hada'ati 'l-ʿuyūn(u), wa Anta Ḥayyun Qayyūm(ul), lā ta'khudhuka sinatuw wa lā nawm(un), Yā Ḥayyu yā Qayyūm(u), ahdi' laylī wa anim ʿaynī.

O Allāh, the stars have gone and the eyes [of people] have sunken [into deep slumber]. Verily You are Everlasting and Eternal, neither sleep, nor slumber can seize you. O Everlasting and Eternal, bless my night with peace and my eyes with sleep (Ibn al-Sunnī).[54]

45. AFTER A FRIGHTENING DREAM OR DISTURBANCE

أَعُوْذُ بِكَلِمَاتِ اللّٰهِ التَّامَّةِ مِنْ غَضَبِهٖ وَشَرِّ عِبَادِهٖ وَمِنْ هَمَزَاتِ الشَّيَاطِيْنِ وَأَنْ يَّحْضُرُوْنِ ❁

A-ʿūdhu bi kalimāti 'Llāhi 't-tāmmāti min ghaḍabihī wa sharri ʿibādihī wa min hamazāti 'sh-shayāṭīni wa ay yaḥḍurūn.

I seek refuge in the perfect words of Allāh against His wrath and the evil of His servants and the evil promptings of devils and against their presence (*Tirmidhī, Mālik*).[55]

46. WHEN HEARING THUNDER

سُبْحَانَ الَّذِيْ يُسَبِّحُ الرَّعْدُ بِحَمْدِهِ وَالْمَلَائِكَةُ مِنْ خِيْفَتِهِ ۞

Subḥāna ʼlladhī yusabbiḥu ʼr-raʿdu bi ḥamdihī wa ʼl-malāʼikatu min khīfatih.

Exalted is He Whom thunder glorifies with praises and so do the angels out of awe for Him (*Mālik*).[56]

47. WHEN AFFLICTED BY AN ILLNESS OR DISEASE

اَللّٰهُمَّ رَبَّ النَّاسِ، أَذْهِبِ الْبَأْسَ، وَاشْفِ أَنْتَ الشَّافِيْ،

لَا شِفَاءَ إِلَّا شِفَاؤُكَ، شِفَاءً لَّا يُغَادِرُ سَقَمًا ۞

Allāhumma Rabba ʼn-nās(i), adhhibi ʼl-baʼsa wa ʼshfi Anta ʼsh-Shāfī, lā shifāʼa illā shifāʼuk(a), shifāʼal lā yughādiru saqamā.

O Allāh, Lord of mankind, remove all harm, and cure, as You are the one Who cures. There is no cure but Your cure: a cure that leaves no illness (*Bukhārī*).[57]

48. WHEN VISITING A PERSON WHO IS ILL

لَا بَأْسَ طَهُوْرٌ إِنْ شَاءَ اللّٰهُ ۞

Lā baʼsa ṭahūrun inshā Allāh.

No need to worry. It [this illness] is purging [of sins], Allāh willing (*Bukhārī*).[58]

49. WHEN CONFRONTED WITH A DIFFICULT SITUATION OR TASK

اَللّٰهُمَّ لَا سَهْلَ إِلَّا مَا جَعَلْتَهُ سَهْلًا، وَّأَنْتَ
تَجْعَلُ الْحُزْنَ إِذَا شِئْتَ سَهْلًا ۞

Allāhumma lā sahla illā mā ja-ʿaltahū sahlan[w],
wa Anta tajʿalu 'l-ḥuzna idhā shi'ta sahlā.

O Allāh, an easy task is only that which You make easy and You make the difficult easy, when You wish (Ibn al-Sunnī).[59]

50. WHAT TO SAY TO A NEWLY-WED COUPLE

بَارَكَ اللّٰهُ لَكَ، وَبَارَكَ عَلَيْكَ، وَجَمَعَ بَيْنَكُمَا فِيْ خَيْرٍ ۞

Bāraka 'Llāhu lak(a), wa bāraka ʿalayk(a),
wa jama-ʿa baynakumā fī khayr.

May Allāh bless you and shower His blessings on you and bring you together in goodness (*Tirmidhī*).[60]

51. WHEN FIRST MEETING ONE'S BRIDE

اَللّٰهُمَّ إِنِّيْ أَسْأَلُكَ خَيْرَهَا وَخَيْرَ مَا جَبَلْتَهَا عَلَيْهِ،
وَأَعُوْذُ بِكَ مِنْ شَرِّهَا وَشَرِّ مَا جَبَلْتَهَا عَلَيْهِ ۞

Allāhumma innī as'aluka khayraha wa khayra
mā jabaltahā ʿalayh(i), wa a-ʿūdhu bika min
sharrihā wa sharri mā jabaltahā ʿalayh.

O Allāh, I ask of You the goodness in her and the good nature upon which You created her and I seek Your protection from the mischief in her and the mischievous nature upon which You created her (*Tirmidhī, Mālik*).[61]

It is also recommended that the husband should hold the forelock or the forehead of the wife and make the following supplication after reciting *Bismillāh*:

بَارَكَ اللّٰهُ لِكُلِّ وَاحِدٍ مِّنَّا فِيْ صَاحِبِهٖ ❁

Bāraka 'Llāhu li kulli wāḥidim minnā fī ṣāḥibih.

May Allāh grant each of us blessing in the other (*Al-Adhkār* from *Abū Dāwūd* and *Ibn Māja*).

52. AT THE COMMENCEMENT OF SEXUAL INTERCOURSE

بِسْمِ اللّٰهِ، اَللّٰهُمَّ جَنِّبْنَا الشَّيْطَانَ وَجَنِّبِ الشَّيْطَانَ مَا رَزَقْتَنَا ❁

Bismi 'Llāh(i), Allāhumma jannibna 'sh-shayṭāna wa jannibi 'sh-shayṭāna mā razaqtanā.

In the name of Allāh. O Allāh, protect us from Satan and keep Satan away from the children You grant us (*Bukhārī*).[62]

53. WHEN A CHILD IS BORN

First call the *adhān* in the right ear and the *iqāma* in the left ear in a moderate voice. Thereafter, supplicate for the child. One may make prayers such as the following:

اَللّٰهُمَّ إِنِّيْ أُعِيْذُهَا (أُعِيْذُهُ m) بِكَ وَذُرِّيَّتَهَا

(وَذُرِّيَّتَهُ m) مِنَ الشَّيْطَانِ الرَّجِيْمِ ❁

Allāhumma innī u-ʿīdhuhā [hū] bika wa dhurriyyatahā [hū] mina 'sh-shayṭāni 'r-rajīm.

O Allāh, I put her [him], and her [his] progeny under Your protection from Satan, the accursed (Qur'ān 3:36).

~

اَللّٰهُمَّ اجْعَلْهُ (هَا) بَرًّا تَقِيًّا، وَّأَنْبِتْهُ (هَا)
فِي الْإِسْلَامِ نَبَاتًا حَسَنًا ❁

Allāhumma 'jʿalhu [hā] barran taqiyyaw wa ambit-hu [hā] fi 'l-Islāmi nabātan ḥasanā.

O Allāh, make him [her] obedient and god fearing, and give him [her] an excellent upbringing in Islam.

~

❁ اَللّٰهُمَّ عَلِّمْهُ (هَا) الْكِتَابَ وَالْحِكْمَةَ وَفَقِّهْهُ (هَا) فِي الدِّيْنِ ❁

Allāhumma ʿallimhu [hā] 'l-kitaba wa 'l-ḥikmata wa faqqihhu [hā] fi 'd-dīn.

O Allāh, teach him [her] the Book and the Wisdom, and bestow on him [her] the understanding of the Religion.

54. SUPPLICATION TO HAVE CHILDREN

رَبِّ لَا تَذَرْنِي فَرْدًا وَأَنتَ خَيْرُ الْوَارِثِينَ ﴿٨٩﴾

Rabbi lā tadharnī fardaw wa Anta Khayru 'l-wārithīn.

O my Lord! Leave me not without offspring; You are the best of inheritors (Qur'ān 21:89).

55. SUPPLICATION TO HAVE A BLESSED FAMILY

رَبَّنَا هَبْ لَنَا مِنْ أَزْوَاجِنَا وَذُرِّيَّاتِنَا قُرَّةَ
أَعْيُنٍ وَاجْعَلْنَا لِلْمُتَّقِينَ إِمَامًا ﴿٧٤﴾

Rabbanā hab lanā min azwājinā wa dhurriyyātinā qurrata aʿyun(iw), wa ʾjʿalnā li ʾl-muttaqīna imāmā.

Our Lord! Grant us spouses and offspring that will be the comfort of our eyes, and make us good examples to the righteous (Qurʾān 25:74).

56. SUPPLICATION FOR A DECEASED CHILD

اَللّٰهُمَّ اجْعَلْهُ (هَاf) لَنَا فَرَطًا وَّسَلَفًا وَّأَجْرًا ❁

Allāhumma ʾjʿalhu [hā] lanā faraṭaw wa salafaw wa ajrā.

O Allāh, make this child a welcomer, forerunner, and a source of recompense for us (*Bukhārī* without chain [*taʿlīqan*] from Ḥasan al-Baṣrī, *Muṣannaf ʿAbd al-Razzāq*).[63]

57. SUPPLICATION FOR A DECEASED MALE OR FEMALE ADULT

اَللّٰهُمَّ اغْفِرْ لِحَيِّنَا وَمَيِّتِنَا، وَشَاهِدِنَا وَغَائِبِنَا، وَصَغِيْرِنَا وَكَبِيْرِنَا،
وَذَكَرِنَا وَأُنْثَانَا. اَللّٰهُمَّ مَنْ أَحْيَيْتَهُ مِنَّا فَأَحْيِهِ عَلَى الْإِسْلَامِ، وَمَنْ
تَوَفَّيْتَهُ مِنَّا فَتَوَفَّهُ عَلَى الْإِيْمَانِ ❁

Allāhumma ʾghfir li ḥayyinā wa mayyitinā, wa shāhidinā wa ghāʾibinā, wa ṣaghīrinā wa kabīrinā, wa dhakarinā wa unthānā.

Allāhumma man aḥyaytahū minnā fa aḥyihī ʿala 'l-islām(i), wa man tawaffaytahū minnā fa tawaffahū ʿala 'l-īmān.

O Allāh, forgive our living and our deceased, our present and absent, our young and old, our men and women. O Allāh, whomever You give life to, let him live in Islam and whomever You give death to, let him die in faith.

The above-mentioned two *duʿās* should be recited after the third *takbīr* in the funeral prayer (*Tirmidhī*).[64]

58. WHEN VISITING THE CEMETERY

اَلسَّلَامُ عَلَيْكُمْ أَهْلَ الدِّيَارِ مِنَ الْمُؤْمِنِيْنَ وَالْمُسْلِمِيْنَ، وَإِنَّا إِنْ شَاءَ اللّٰهُ بِكُمْ لَلَاحِقُوْنَ، أَسْأَلُ اللّٰهَ لَنَا وَلَكُمُ الْعَافِيَةَ ❁

As-salāmu ʿalaykum ahla 'd-diyyāri mina 'l-mu'minīna wa 'l-muslimīn(a), wa innā inshā Allāhu bikum la lāḥiqūn(a), as'alu 'Llāha lanā wa lakumu 'l-ʿāfiyah.

Peace be upon you, O dwellers of this place—Believers and Muslims. Verily when Allāh wills we will join you. I ask Allāh for our and your safety (*Muslim*).[65]

59. WHEN SATAN PLACES DOUBTS REGARDING ONE'S FAITH

أَعُوْذُ بِاللّٰهِ مِنَ الشَّيْطَانِ الرَّجِيْمِ. آمَنْتُ بِاللّٰهِ ❁

A-ʿūdhu bi 'Llāhi mina 'sh-shayṭāni 'r-rajīm(i). Āmantu bi 'Llāh.

I seek refuge in Allāh from Satan the accursed. I believe in Allāh (*Muslim*).[66]

60. WHEN ASKING FOR THE HONOR OF MARTYRDOM (*SHAHĀDA*)

اَللّٰهُمَّ ارْزُقْنِيْ شَهَادَةً فِيْ سَبِيْلِكَ، وَاجْعَلْ

مَوْتِيْ فِيْ بَلَدِ رَسُوْلِكَ ❁

Allāhumma ʾrzuqnī shahādatan fī sabīlik(a),
wa ʾjʿal mawtī fī baladi Rasūlik.

O Allāh, grant me martyrdom in Your path and let me die in the city of Your Messenger (*Bukhārī*).[67]

Part 3

جامع الدعوات

Comprehensive Supplications

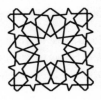

Comprehensive Supplications from the Qur'ān

رَبَّنَا تَقَبَّلْ مِنَّا ۖ إِنَّكَ أَنْتَ السَّمِيعُ الْعَلِيمُ ﴿١٢٧﴾

Rabbanā taqabbal minnā innaka Anta 'ṣ-Samī-ʿu 'l-ʿAlīm.

Our Lord! Accept (this worship) from us; You are the All-Hearing, the All-Knowing (2:127).

~

رَبَّنَا وَاجْعَلْنَا مُسْلِمَيْنِ لَكَ وَمِنْ ذُرِّيَّتِنَا أُمَّةً مُسْلِمَةً لَكَ وَأَرِنَا
مَنَاسِكَنَا وَتُبْ عَلَيْنَا ۖ إِنَّكَ أَنْتَ التَّوَّابُ الرَّحِيمُ ﴿١٢٨﴾

Rabbanā wa 'jʿalnā muslimayni laka wa min dhurriyyatinā ummatam muslimatal lak(a), wa arinā manāsikanā wa tub ʿalaynā, innaka Anta 't-Tawwābu 'r-Raḥīm.

Our Lord! Make us submissive to You, and of our offspring a nation submissive to You, Show us our rites, and turn to us [in Mercy]. You are the Oft-Forgiving, the Most Merciful (2:128).

~

رَبَّنَا أَفْرِغْ عَلَيْنَا صَبْرًا وَثَبِّتْ أَقْدَامَنَا
وَانْصُرْنَا عَلَى الْقَوْمِ الْكَافِرِينَ ﴿٢٥٠﴾

Rabbanā afrigh ʿalynā ṣabraw wa thabbit aqdāmanā wa 'nṣurnā ʿala 'l-qawmi 'l-kāfirīn.

Our Lord! Pour patience upon us and make firm our feet, and help us against the unbelieving people (2:250).

~

رَبَّنَا آتِنَا فِي الدُّنْيَا حَسَنَةً وَفِي الْآخِرَةِ حَسَنَةً وَقِنَا عَذَابَ النَّارِ ﴿٢٠١﴾

Rabbanā ātinā fi 'd-dunyā ḥasanataw wa fī 'l-ākhiratī ḥasanatan[w], wa qinā ʿadhāba 'n-nār.

Our Lord! Give us good in this world and good in the Hereafter, and protect us from the torment of the Fire! (2:201).

~

رَبَّنَا لَا تُزِغْ قُلُوبَنَا بَعْدَ إِذْ هَدَيْتَنَا وَهَبْ لَنَا مِن لَّدُنْكَ رَحْمَةً ۚ إِنَّكَ أَنْتَ الْوَهَّابُ ﴿٨﴾

Rabbanā lā tuzigh qulūbanā baʿda idh hadaytanā wa hab lanā mil ladunka raḥma(tan), innaka Anta 'l-Wahhāb.

Our Lord! Let not our hearts stray now that You have guided us, but grant us mercy from Your Own Presence, for You are the Giver [of bounties without measure] (3:8).

~

رَبَّنَا إِنَّنَا آمَنَّا فَاغْفِرْ لَنَا ذُنُوبَنَا وَقِنَا عَذَابَ النَّارِ ﴿١٦﴾

Rabbanā innanā āmannā fa 'ghfir lanā dhunūbanā wa qinā ʿadhāba 'n-nār.

Our Lord! We believe. Forgive us our sins, and save us from the torment of the Fire (3:16).

~

رَبِّ هَبْ لِي مِن لَّدُنْكَ ذُرِّيَّةً طَيِّبَةً ۖ إِنَّكَ سَمِيعُ الدُّعَاءِ ﴿٣٨﴾

Rabbi hab lī mil ladunka dhurriyatan ṭayyibatan innaka Samī-ʿu 'd-du-ʿā.

My Lord! Grant me from You goodly offspring.
Verily, You hear all prayers (3:38).

رَبَّنَا اغْفِرْ لَنَا ذُنُوبَنَا وَإِسْرَافَنَا فِي أَمْرِنَا
وَثَبِّتْ أَقْدَامَنَا وَانْصُرْنَا عَلَى الْقَوْمِ الْكَافِرِينَ ﴿١٤٧﴾

Rabbanā 'ghfir lanā dhunūbanā wa isrāfanā fī amrinā wa thabbit aqdāmanā wa 'nṣurnā ʿalā 'l-qawmi 'l-kāfirīn.

Our Lord, forgive us our sins and any transgressions
in our affair, make firm our feet and help us
against the unbelieving people (3:147).

رَبَّنَا وَآتِنَا مَا وَعَدْتَنَا عَلَىٰ رُسُلِكَ وَلَا تُخْزِنَا
يَوْمَ الْقِيَامَةِ ۗ إِنَّكَ لَا تُخْلِفُ الْمِيعَادَ ﴿١٩٤﴾

Rabbanā wa ātinā mā waʿattanā ʿalā rusulik(a), wa lā tukhzinā yawma 'l-qiyāmati innaka lā tukhlifu 'l-mī-ʿād.

Our Lord! Grant us what You promised to us through Your Messengers, and save us from shame on the Day of Judgment, for You never break Your promise (3:194).

رَبَّنَا ظَلَمْنَا أَنفُسَنَا وَإِن لَّمْ تَغْفِرْ لَنَا وَتَرْحَمْنَا
لَنَكُونَنَّ مِنَ الْخَاسِرِينَ ﴿٢٣﴾

Rabbanā ẓalamnā anfusanā wa il lam taghfir lanā
wa tarḥamnā la nakūnanna mina 'l-khāsirīn.

Our Lord! We have wronged ourselves, and
if You do not forgive us and have mercy upon
us we shall be among the lost (7:23).

~

رَبِّ اجْعَلْنِي مُقِيمَ الصَّلَاةِ وَمِن ذُرِّيَّتِي رَبَّنَا وَتَقَبَّلْ دُعَاءِ ﴿٤٠﴾ رَبَّنَا
اغْفِرْ لِي وَلِوَالِدَيَّ وَلِلْمُؤْمِنِينَ يَوْمَ يَقُومُ الْحِسَابُ ﴿٤١﴾

Rabbi 'jʿalnī muqīma 'ṣ-ṣalāti wa min dhurriyyatī Rabbanā wa taqabbal du-ʿā'(i), Rabbanā 'ghfir lī wa li wālidayya wa li 'l-mu'minīna yawma yaqūmu 'l-ḥisāb.

My Lord, make me one who establishes prayer, and of my offspring. Our Lord, accept my prayer. Our Lord, forgive me and my parents and the believers on the Day reckoning is made (14:40–41).

~

لَا إِلَٰهَ إِلَّا أَنتَ سُبْحَانَكَ إِنِّي كُنتُ مِنَ الظَّالِمِينَ ﴿٨٧﴾

Lā ilāha illā Anta subḥānaka innī kuntu mina 'ẓ-ẓālimīn.

There is no god but You, Exalted are You,
indeed I was of the oppressors (21:87).

~

رَبَّنَا عَلَيْكَ تَوَكَّلْنَا وَإِلَيْكَ أَنَبْنَا وَإِلَيْكَ الْمَصِيرُ ﴿٤﴾

Rabbanā ʿalayka tawakkalnā wa ilayka anabnā wa ilayka ʾl-maṣīr.

Our Lord! In You we trust, to You we turn, and to You is the final return (60:4).

~

رَبَّنَا لَا تَجْعَلْنَا فِتْنَةً لِّلَّذِينَ كَفَرُوا وَاغْفِرْ لَنَا

رَبَّنَا ۖ إِنَّكَ أَنتَ الْعَزِيزُ الْحَكِيمُ ﴿٥﴾

Rabbanā lā tajʿalnā fitnatal li ʾlladhīna kafarū wa ʾghfir lanā Rabbanā, innaka Anta ʾl-ʿAzīzu ʾl-Ḥakīm.

Our Lord! Make us not a trial for the unbelievers, and forgive us, our Lord! Indeed You are the Exalted in Might, the Wise (60:5).

~

سُبْحَانَ رَبِّكَ رَبِّ الْعِزَّةِ عَمَّا يَصِفُونَ ﴿١٨٠﴾ وَسَلَامٌ عَلَى

الْمُرْسَلِينَ ﴿١٨١﴾ وَالْحَمْدُ لِلَّهِ رَبِّ الْعَالَمِينَ ﴿١٨٢﴾

Subḥāna Rabbika Rabbi ʾl-ʿizzati ʿāmmā yaṣifūn(a), wa salāmun ʿalā ʾl-mursalīn(a), wa ʾl-ḥamdu li ʾLlāhi Rabbi ʾl-ʿālamīn.

Exalted is Your Lord, the Lord of Glory, above what they ascribe [to Him]. Peace be upon the Messengers, and Praise be to Allāh, the Lord of the Worlds (37:180–182).

Comprehensive Supplications from the Ḥadīth

اَللّٰهُمَّ إِنِّيْ أَسْأَلُكَ الْهُدٰى وَالتُّقٰى وَالْعَفَافَ وَالْغِنٰى ❁

Allāhumma innī as'aluka 'l-hudā wa 'ttuqā wa 'l-ʿafāfa wa 'l-ghinā.

O Allāh, I ask of You guidance, piety, chastity and independence [from your creation] (*Muslim*).[68]

~

اَللّٰهُمَّ مُصَرِّفَ الْقُلُوْبِ، صَرِّفْ قُلُوْبَنَا عَلٰى طَاعَتِكَ ❁

Allāhumma Muṣarrifa 'l-qulūb(i), ṣarrif qulūbanā ʿalā ṭā-ʿatik.

O Allāh, Turner of hearts, turn our hearts toward Your obedience (*Muslim*).[69]

~

يَا مُقَلِّبَ الْقُلُوْبِ، ثَبِّتْ قَلْبِيْ عَلٰى دِيْنِكَ ❁

Yā Muqalliba 'l-qulūb(i), thabbit qalbī ʿalā dīnik.

O Controller of the hearts, make my heart firm in Your Religion (*Tirmidhī, Mustadrak*).[70]

~

اَللّٰهُمَّ أٰتِنَا فِي الدُّنْيَا حَسَنَةً وَّفِي الْأٰخِرَةِ حَسَنَةً وَّقِنَا عَذَابَ النَّارِ ❁

Allāhumma ātinā fi 'd-dunyā ḥasanataw wa fi 'l-ākhirati ḥasanataw wa qinā ʿadhāba 'n-nār.

O Allāh, grant us good in this world and good in

the Hereafter and save us from the punishment
of the Hellfire (*Bukhārī, Muslim*).[71]

اَللّٰهُمَّ إِنِّيْ أَعُوْذُ بِكَ مِنَ الْعَجْزِ، وَالْكَسَلِ، وَالْجُبْنِ،
وَالْهَرَمِ، وَالْبُخْلِ، وَأَعُوْذُ بِكَ مِنْ عَذَابِ الْقَبْرِ،
وَأَعُوْذُ بِكَ مِنْ فِتْنَةِ الْمَحْيَا وَالْمَمَاتِ ❁

Allāhumma innī a-ʿūdhu bika mina 'l-ʿajz(i), wa
'l-kasal(i), wa 'l-jubn(i), wa 'l-haram(i), wa 'l-bukhl(i),
wa a-ʿūdhu bika min ʿadhābi 'l-qabr(i), wa a-ʿudhu
bika min fitnati 'l-maḥyā wa 'l-mamāt.

O Allāh, I seek Your protection from inability, laziness, cowardice, decrepitude; and miserliness; and I seek Your protection from the punishment of the grave; and I seek Your protection from the mischief of life and death (*Bukhārī*).[72]

اَللّٰهُمَّ إِنَّا نَسْأَلُكَ مِنْ خَيْرِ مَا سَأَلَكَ مِنْهُ نَبِيُّكَ مُحَمَّدٌ صَلَّى اللّٰهُ
عَلَيْهِ وَسَلَّمَ، وَنَعُوْذُ بِكَ مِنْ شَرِّ مَا اسْتَعَاذَكَ مِنْهُ نَبِيُّكَ مُحَمَّدٌ صَلَّى
اللّٰهُ عَلَيْهِ وَسَلَّمَ، وَأَنْتَ الْمُسْتَعَانُ وَعَلَيْكَ الْبَلَاغُ، وَلَا حَوْلَ وَلَا
قُوَّةَ إِلَّا بِاللّٰهِ ❁

Allāhumma innā nas'aluka min khayri mā sa'alaka minhu nabiyyuka Muḥammadun ṣalla 'Llāhu ʿalayhi wa sallam(a), wa na-ʿūdhu bika min sharri ma 'sta-ʿādhaka minhu nabiyyuka Muḥammadun ṣalla 'Llāhu ʿalayhi wa sallam(a), wa Anta 'l-Musta-ʿānu wa ʿalayka 'l-balāgh(u), wa lā ḥawla wa lā quwwata illā bi 'Llāh.

O Allāh, we ask of You all the good things asked of You by Your Prophet Muḥammad ﷺ and We seek Your protection from all the evil things from which Your Prophet Muḥammad ﷺ sought Your protection. You are the One Whose help is sought, and Yours is the final argument, and there is no power [to do good] or strength [to avoid evil] but with Allāh (*Tirmidhī*).[73]

اَللّٰهُمَّ إِنَّا نَسْأَلُكَ مُوْجِبَاتِ رَحْمَتِكَ، وَعَزَائِمَ مَغْفِرَتِكَ، وَالسَّلَامَةَ مِنْ كُلِّ إِثْمٍ، وَّالْغَنِيْمَةَ مِنْ كُلِّ بِرٍّ، وَّالْفَوْزَ بِالْجَنَّةِ وَالنَّجَاةَ مِنَ النَّارِ ۞

Allāhumma innā nas'aluka mūjibāti raḥmatik(a), wa ʿazā'ima maghfiratik(a), wa 's-salāmata min kulli ithm(in), wa 'l-ghanīmata min kulli birr(in), wa 'l-fawza bi 'l-jannati wa 'n-najāta mina 'n-nār.

O Allāh, I ask of You those things which will procure Your mercy, and I ask for Your immense forgiveness, and I ask for complete safety from [committing] sins, and a full share of virtuous deeds, and salvation by attaining Paradise and deliverance from Hell (*Mustadrak*).[74]

اَللّٰهُمَّ إِنِّيْ أَسْأَلُكَ الْعَفْوَ وَالْعَافِيَةَ فِيْ دِيْنِي وَدُنْيَايَ وَأَهْلِيْ وَمَالِيْ ۞

Allāhumma innī as'aluka 'l-ʿafwa wa 'l-ʿāfiyata fī dīnī wa dunyāya wa ahlī wa mālī.

O Allāh, I seek Your forgiveness and wellbeing in my religion, my worldly life, my family, and my wealth (*Mustadrak*).[75]

اَللّٰهُمَّ إِنِّيْ أَسْأَلُكَ حُبَّكَ، وَحُبَّ مَن يُّحِبُّكَ،
وَالْعَمَلَ الَّذِيْ يُبَلِّغُنِيْ حُبَّكَ ❁

Allāhumma innī as'aluka ḥubbak(a), wa ḥubba may yuḥibbuk(a), wa 'l-ʿamala 'lladhī yuballighunī ḥubbak.

O Allāh, I beg of You Your love and the love of those who love You and I ask of You such deeds which will bring me Your love (*Tirmidhī*).[76]

اَللّٰهُمَّ أَعِنِّيْ عَلٰى ذِكْرِكَ وَشُكْرِكَ وَحُسْنِ عِبَادَتِكَ ❁

Allāhumma a-ʿinnī ʿalā dhikrika wa shukrika wa ḥusni ʿibādatik.

O Allāh, help me in Your remembrance, Your thanks, and in perfecting Your prescribed worship (*Tirmidhī*).[77]

اَللّٰهُمَّ إِنِّيْ أَسْأَلُكَ عِلْمًا نَّافِعًا وَّرِزْقًا طَيِّبًا وَّعَمَلًا مُّتَقَبَّلًا ❁

Allāhumma innī as'aluka ʿilman nāfi-ʿaw wa rizqan ṭayyibaw wa ʿamalam mutaqabbalā.

O Allāh, I ask of You beneficial knowledge, and goodly sustenance, and accepted acts of worship (*Ibn Māja*).

اَللّٰهُمَّ إِنِّيْ أَعُوْذُ بِكَ مِنْ عَذَابِ الْقَبْرِ، وَأَعُوْذُ بِكَ مِنْ فِتْنَةِ الْمَسِيْحِ الدَّجَّالِ، وَأَعُوْذُ بِكَ مِنْ فِتْنَةِ الْمَحْيٰ وَالْمَمَاتِ، اَللّٰهُمَّ إِنِّي أَعُوْذُ بِكَ مِنَ الْمَأْثَمِ وَالْمَغْرَمِ ۞

Allāhumma innī a-ʿūdhu bika min ʿadhābi 'l-qabr(i), wa a-ʿūdhu bika min fitnati 'l-masīḥi 'd-dajjāl(i), wa a-ʿudhu bika min fitnati 'l-maḥyā wa 'l-mamāt(i). Allāhumma innī a-ʿudhu bika mina 'l-ma'thami wa 'l-maghram.

O Allāh, I seek your protection from the torment of the grave, and I seek your protection from the mischief of the False Messiah, and I seek Your protection from the trials of this life and death. O Allāh, I seek Your protection from sin and debt (*Bukhārī*).

~

اَللّٰهُمَّ إِنِّيْ أَسْئَلُكَ مِنَ الْخَيْرِ كُلِّهٖ، عَاجِلِهٖ وَآجِلِهٖ، مَا عَلِمْتُ مِنْهُ وَمَا لَمْ أَعْلَمْ، وأَعُوْذُ بِكَ مِنَ النَّارِ وَمَا قَرَّبَ إِلَيْهِ مِنْ قَوْلٍ أَوْ عَمَلٍ ۞

Allāhumma innī as'aluka mina 'l-khayri kullih(ī), ʿājilihī wa ājilih(ī), mā ʿalimtu minhu wa mā lam aʿlam, wa a-ʿudhu bika mina 'n-nāri wa mā qarraba ilayhi min qawlin aw ʿamal.

O Allāh, I ask of You all good whether it comes soon or late, whether I know it or not, and I seek your protection from the Fire and all acts of word or deed that may lead me to it (*Aḥmad, Mustadrak*).

~

يَا حَيُّ يَا قَيُّومُ بِرَحْمَتِكَ أَسْتَغِيْثُ، أَصْلِحْ لِيْ شَأْنِيْ كُلَّهُ، وَلَا تَكِلْنِيْ إِلٰى نَفْسِيْ طَرْفَةَ عَيْنٍ ❁

Yā Ḥayyu ya Qayyūmu bi raḥmatika astaghīth(u), aṣliḥ lī sha'nī kullah(ū) wa lā takilnī ilā nafsī ṭarfata ʿayn.

O You the Everlasting and All-Sustainer I fervently call upon Your mercy so that You may set right all my affairs and may not leave me to myself for the blink of an eye (*Mustadrak*).

~

اَللّٰهُمَّ اجْعَلْ فِيْ قَلْبِيْ نُوْرًا وَّفِيْ لِسَانِيْ نُوْرًا وَّفِيْ بَصَرِيْ نُوْرًا، وَاجْعَلْ فِيْ سَمْعِيْ نُوْرًا وَّعَن يَّمِيْنِيْ نُوْرًا وَّعَن يَّسَارِيْ نُوْرًا، وَّفَوْقِيْ نُوْرًا وَّتَحْتِيْ نُوْرًا، وَّأَمَامِيْ نُوْرًا وَّخَلْفِيْ نُوْرًا، وَّاجْعَل لِّيْ نُوْرًا ❁

Allāhumma 'jʿal fī qalbī nūraw wa fī lisānī nūraw wa fī baṣarī nūran[w], wa 'jʿal fī samʿī nūraw wa ʿan yamīnī nūraw wa ʿay yasārī nūran[w], wa ʿan fawqī nuraw wa taḥtī nūraw wa amāmī nūraw wa khalfī nūran[w], wa 'jʿal lī nūrā.

O Allāh, pour your light into my heart, my tongue, my eyes, my ears, and put it on my right, my left, behind me, before me, beneath me and above me, and grant me light (*Bukhārī, Muslim*).

~

اَللّٰهُمَّ لَكَ الْحَمْدُ أَنْتَ نُوْرُ السَّمٰوَاتِ وَالْأَرْضِ وَمَنْ فِيْهِنَّ، وَلَكَ

الْحَمْدُ أَنْتَ قَيِّمُ السَّمٰوَاتِ وَالْأَرْضِ وَمَنْ فِيهِنَّ، وَلَكَ الْحَمْدُ أَنْتَ الْحَقُّ وَوَعْدُكَ الْحَقُّ وَقَوْلُكَ الْحَقُّ وَلِقَائُكَ حَقٌّ وَّالْجَنَّةُ حَقٌّ وَّالنَّارُ حَقٌّ وَّالسَّاعَةُ حَقٌّ، اَللّٰهُمَّ لَكَ أَسْلَمْتُ وَبِكَ آمَنْتُ وَعَلَيْكَ تَوَكَّلْتُ وَإِلَيْكَ أَنَبْتُ وَبِكَ خَاصَمْتُ وَإِلَيْكَ حَاكَمْتُ، فَاغْفِرْ لِي مَا قَدَّمْتُ وَأَخَّرْتُ وَأَسْرَرْتُ وَأَعْلَنْتُ، أَنْتَ إِلٰهِيْ لَا إِلٰهَ إِلَّا أَنْتَ ❁

Allāhumma laka 'l-ḥamdu Anta Nūru 's-samawāti wa 'l-arḍi wa man fīhinn(a), wa laka 'l-ḥamdu Anta Qayyimu 's-samāwāti wa 'l-arḍī wa man fīhinn(a), wa laka 'l-ḥamdu Anta 'l-Ḥaqqu wa waᶜduka 'l-ḥaqqu wa qawluka 'l-ḥaqqu wa liqa'uka ḥaqquw wa 'l-jannatu ḥaqquw wa 'n-nāru ḥaqquw wa 's-sāᶜatu ḥaqq(un). Allāhumma laka aslamtu wa bika āmantu wa ᶜalayka tawakkaltu wa ilayka anabtu wa bika khāṣamtu wa ilayka ḥākamt(u), fa 'ghfir lī mā qaddamtu wa akhkhartu wa asrartu wa aᶜlant(u), Anta Ilāhī lā ilāha illā Ant.

O Allāh, to You is praise. You are the light of the heavens and the earth and of all those therein. To You is praise, You are the caretaker of the heavens and the earth and of all those therein. To You is praise, You are the Truth, and Your promise is true, and Your word is true, and meeting You is true, and Paradise is true, and Hell is true, and the Hour is true. O Allāh, to You I submit, in You I believe, in You I place my trust, to You I turn, with You I confront [my enemies], and to You I entrust my case; so forgive me my sins, those I have committed and those I have yet to commit, those I concealed and those I made manifest. You are my Lord, there is no God but You.

This *duʿā'* should also be recited when one wakes for *Tahajjud* prayer, as was the practice of the Messenger of Allāh ﷺ (*Bukhārī, Muslim*).

اَللّٰهُمَّ أَصْلِحْ لِيْ دِيْنِيَ الَّذِيْ هُوَ عِصْمَةُ أَمْرِيْ، وَأَصْلِحْ لِيْ دُنْيَايَ
الَّتِيْ فِيْهَا مَعَاشِيْ، وَأَصْلِحْ لِيْ آخِرَتِيَ الَّتِيْ فِيْهَا مَعَادِيْ، وَاجْعَلِ
الْحَيَاةَ زِيَادَةً لِّيْ فِيْ كُلِّ خَيْرٍ، وَّاجْعَلِ الْمَوْتَ رَاحَةً لِّيْ مِنْ كُلِّ شَرٍّ

Allāhumma aṣliḥ lī dīniya 'lladhī huwa ʿiṣmatu amrī, wa aṣliḥ lī dunyāya 'llatī fīhā ma-ʿāshī, wa aṣliḥ lī ākhiratiya 'llatī fīhā ma-ʿādī, wa 'jʿali 'l-ḥayāta ziyaddatal lī fī kulli khayr(in), wa 'jʿali 'l-mawta rāḥatal lī min kulli sharr.

O Allāh, set aright my religious life which is a safeguard in all my affairs, set aright my worldly life in which is my subsistence, set aright my Hereafter unto which I return, and make my life a source of increase in all good, and make my death a refuge from every evil (*Muslim*).

Part 4

الأوراد المخصوصة

Other Specific Prayers

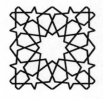

1. *SAYYID AL-ISTIGHFĀR* (THE GREATEST PRAYER FOR FORGIVENESS)

اَللّٰهُمَّ أَنْتَ رَبِّيْ لَا إِلٰهَ إِلَّا أَنْتَ، خَلَقْتَنِيْ وَأَنَا عَبْدُكَ، وَأَنَا عَلٰى عَهْدِكَ وَوَعْدِكَ مَا اسْتَطَعْتُ، أَعُوْذُ بِكَ مِنْ شَرِّ مَا صَنَعْتُ، أَبُوْءُ لَكَ بِنِعْمَتِكَ عَلَيَّ، وَأَبُوْءُ بِذَنْبِيْ، فَاغْفِرْ لِيْ فَإِنَّهُ لَا يَغْفِرُ الذُّنُوْبَ إِلَّا أَنْتَ ✿

Allāhumma Anta Rabbī lā ilāha illā Ant(a), khalaqtanī wa ana ʿabduk(a), wa ana ʿalā ʿahdika wa waʿdika ma ʾstaṭaʿt(u), a-ʿūdhu bika min sharri mā ṣanaʿt(u), abū'u laka bi niʿmatika ʿalayy(a), wa abū'u bi dhambī, fa ʾghfir lī fa innahū lā yaghfiru ʾdh-dhunūba illā Ant.

O Allāh, You are my Lord. There is no god but You. You have created me and I am Your servant and as far as possible I abide by Your promise and covenant (which I made with You). I seek Your protection against the consequences of my wrongdoings. I fully acknowledge the grace You have bestowed upon me and confess my faults. So pardon me as none besides You can pardon sins.

Whoever recites this during the day or night with firm belief, then happens to pass away before the next evening or morning, he will be counted among the dwellers of Paradise (*Bukhārī*).[78]

2. *QUNŪT AL-NĀZILA* (PRAYER DURING CALAMITY)

When the general Muslim public in any part of the world, is afflicted with a calamity, the *Qunūt al-Nāzila* should be recited in the Fajr prayer. The procedure is that the *imām* stands with his followers after the *rukūʿ* in the second *rakʿa,* everyone keeping their arms by their sides (Ḥanafī school) or raising them to the chest (Shāfiʿī school). The *imām* then recites the prayer below and the followers say *āmīn* silently, after which they all go into prostration as usual.

اَللّٰهُمَّ اهْدِنِيْ فِيْمَنْ هَدَيْتَ، وَعَافِنِيْ فِيْمَنْ عَافَيْتَ، وَتَوَلَّنِيْ فِيْمَنْ تَوَلَّيْتَ، وَبَارِكْ لِيْ فِيْمَا أَعْطَيْتَ، وَقِنِيْ شَرَّ مَا قَضَيْتَ، فَإِنَّكَ تَقْضِيْ وَلَا يُقْضٰى عَلَيْكَ، وَإِنَّهٗ لَا يَذِلُّ مَن وَّالَيْتَ، تَبَارَكْتَ رَبَّنَا وَتَعَالَيْتَ ❁

Allāhumma 'hdinī fī man hadayt(a), wa ʿāfinī fī man ʿāfayt(a), wa tawallanī fī man tawallayt(a), wa bārik lī fī mā aʿṭayt(a), wa qinī sharra mā qaḍayt(a), fa innaka taqḍī wa lā yuqḍā ʿalayk(a), wa innahū lā yadhillu maw wālayt(a), tabārakta Rabbanā wa ta-ʿālayt.

O Allāh, Guide me aright among those You guide aright, and grant me health and pardon among those You grant health and pardon, and care for me among those You care for, and bless me in what You have given, and protect me from the evil of what You have predestined. You alone decree and none decrees against You. He is not abased whom You befriend. Blessed are You our Lord and You are Most High (*Abū Dāwūd, Nasā'ī, Tirmidhī*).[79]

Then recite:

اَللّٰهُمَّ اغْفِرْ لِلْمُؤْمِنِيْنَ وَالْمُؤْمِنَاتِ، وَالْمُسْلِمِيْنَ وَالْمُسْلِمَاتِ، وَأَلِّفْ بَيْنَ قُلُوْبِهِمْ، وَأَصْلِحْ ذَاتَ بَيْنِهِمْ، وَانْصُرْهُمْ عَلٰى عَدُوِّكَ

وَعَلٰى عَدُوِّهِمْ، اَللّٰهُمَّ الْعَنْ كَفَرَةَ أَهْلِ الْكِتَابِ الَّذِيْنَ يُكَذِّبُوْنَ
رُسُلَكَ، وَيُقَاتِلُوْنَ أَوْلِيَائَكَ، اَللّٰهُمَّ خَالِفْ بَيْنَ كَلِمَتِهِمْ، وَزَلْزِلْ
أَقْدَامَهُمْ، وَأَنْزِلْ بِهِمْ بَأْسَكَ الَّذِيْ لَا تَرُدُّهٗ عَنِ الْقَوْمِ الْمُجْرِمِيْنَ ۞

Allāhumma ’ghfir li ’l-mu’minīna wa ’l-mu’mināt(i), wa ’l-muslimīna wa ’l-muslimāt(i), wa allif bayna qulūbihim, wa aṣliḥ dhāta baynihim, wa ’nṣurhum ʿalā ʿaduwwika wa ʿalā ʿaduwwihim, Allāhumma ’lʿan kafarata ahli ’l-kitābi ’lladhīna yukadhdhibūna Rusulak(a), wa yuqātilūna awliyā’ak(a), Allāhumma khālif bayna kalimatihim, wa zalzil aqdāmahum, wa anzil bihim ba’saka ’lladhī lā tarudduhū ʿani ’l-qawmi ’l-mujrimīn.

O Allāh forgive all the believers, men and women, and all Muslims, men and women. Unite their hearts in mutual love, and set aright their mutual affairs, and help them against Your and their enemies. O Allāh curse the unbelievers among the people of the book who belie the Prophets and who fight Your chosen ones. O Allāh divide them, and make their feet tremble, and send down upon them Your punishment, which You do not turn away from the people of sin (*Muṣannaf ʿAbd al-Razzāq*).[80]

3. SUPPLICATION (*QUNŪT*) TO BE MADE IN *WITR* PRAYER

اَللّٰهُمَّ إِنَّا نَسْتَعِيْنُكَ وَنَسْتَغْفِرُكَ وَنُؤْمِنُ بِكَ وَنُثْنِيْ عَلَيْكَ الْخَيْرَ،
وَنَشْكُرُكَ وَلَا نَكْفُرُكَ، وَ نَخْلَعُ وَ نَتْرُكُ مَنْ يَّفْجُرُكَ، اَللّٰهُمَّ إِيَّاكَ
نَعْبُدُ وَلَكَ نُصَلِّيْ وَنَسْجُدُ، وَإِلَيْكَ نَسْعٰى وَنَحْفِدُ، وَنَخْشٰى
عَذَابَكَ وَنَرْجُوْ رَحْمَتَكَ، إِنَّ عَذَابَكَ الْجِدَّ بِالْكُفَّارِ مُلْحِقٌ ۞

Allāhumma innā nasta-ʿīnuka wa nastaghfiruka wa nu'minu bika wa nuthnī ʿalayka 'l-khayr(a), wa nashkuruka wa lā nakfuruk(a), wa nakhla-ʿu wa natruku may yafjuruk(a), Allāhumma iyyāka naʿbudu wa laka nuṣallī wa nasjud(u), wa ilayka nasʿā wa naḥfid(u), wa nakhshā ʿadhābaka wa narjū raḥmatak(a), innā ʿadhābaka 'l-jidda bi 'l-kuffāri mulḥiq.

O Allāh, we seek Your assistance, and we ask for Your forgiveness, and we believe in You, and we praise You for all good, and we are grateful to You, and we part with and break away from all who disobey You. O Allāh, You alone do we worship, and to You we pray and prostrate, and we hasten eagerly toward You, and we fear Your punishment, and we hope for Your mercy. Indeed Your severe punishment is surely to be meted out to the unbelievers (*Muṣannaf Ibn Abī Shayba*).[81]

This supplication is made in the third *rakʿa* of *witr* prayer after raising the hands and saying the *takbīr.*

4. SUPPLICATION TO BE MADE AFTER *WITR* PRAYER

سُبْحَانَ الْمَلِكِ الْقُدُّوْسِ ❁

Subḥāna 'l-Maliki 'l-Quddūs.

Exalted is the Sovereign, the Holy.

Recite it thrice, the third time aloud prolonging the final syllable of the word Quddūs (*Nasā'ī*).[82]

5. SUPPLICATION BETWEEN THE TWO PROSTRATIONS

اَللّٰهُمَّ اغْفِرْ لِيْ وَارْحَمْنِيْ وَعَافِنِيْ وَاهْدِنِيْ وَارْزُقْنِيْ ۞

Allāhumma ʼghfir lī wa ʼr-ḥamnī wa ʿāfinī wahdinī warzuqnī.

O Allāh, forgive me, have mercy on me, grant me good health, guide me, and grant me sustenance (*Abū Dāwūd*).[83]

6. SUPPLICATION IN THE FINAL SITTING OF THE PRAYER

اَللّٰهُمَّ إِنِّيْ ظَلَمْتُ نَفْسِيْ ظُلْمًا كَثِيْرًا، وَّلَا يَغْفِرُ الذُّنُوْبَ إِلَّا أَنْتَ،

فَاغْفِرْ لِيْ مَغْفِرَةً مِّنْ عِنْدَكَ وَارْحَمْنِيْ، إِنَّكَ أَنْتَ الْغَفُوْرُ الرَّحِيْمُ ۞

Allāhumma innī ẓalamtu nafsī ẓulman kathīran[w], wa lā yaghfiru ʼdh-dhunūba illā Ant(a), fa ʼghfir lī maghfiratam min ʿindika wa ʼr-ḥamnī, innaka Anta ʼl-Ghafūru ʼr-Raḥim.

O Allāh, verily I have greatly wronged myself, none but You can forgive sins, so forgive me with forgiveness from Yourself and have mercy on me. Verily You are All-Forgiving and Merciful (*Bukhārī*).[84]

This supplication is made following the salutations (*ṣalawāt*) on the Messenger of Allāh ﷺ in the final sitting of prayer.

7. SUPPLICATIONS FOLLOWING THE OBLIGATORY PRAYERS

First recite the prayer for forgiveness (*istighfār*) thrice,

أَسْتَغْفِرُ اللّٰهَ ۞

Astaghfiru ʼLlāh. I seek forgiveness from Allāh.

Then recite:

اَللّٰهُمَّ أَنْتَ السَّلَامُ، وَمِنْكَ السَّلَامُ،

تَبَارَكْتَ يَا ذَا الْجَلَالِ وَالْإِكْرَامِ ۞

Allāhumma Anta 's-Salām(u), wa minka 's-salām(u),
tabārakta yā Dha 'l-jalāli wa 'l-ikrām.

O Allāh, You are the Giver of Peace and peace comes from You alone. You are blessed, O Majestic and Benevolent (*Muslim*).[85]

Also recite:

لَا إِلٰهَ إِلَّا اللّٰهُ وَحْدَهُ لَا شَرِيْكَ لَهُ، لَهُ الْمُلْكُ وَلَهُ الْحَمْدُ وَهُوَ عَلٰى كُلِّ شَيْءٍ قَدِيْرٌ. اَللّٰهُمَّ لَا مَانِعَ لِمَا أَعْطَيْتَ، وَلَا مُعْطِيَ لِمَا مَنَعْتَ، وَلَا يَنْفَعُ ذَا الْجَدِّ مِنْكَ الْجَدُّ ۞

Lā ilāha illa 'Llāhu waḥdahū lā sharīka lah(ū), lahu 'l-mulku wa lahu 'l-ḥamdu wa Huwa ʿalā kulli shay'in Qadīr(un). Allāhumma lā māni-ʿa limā aʿṭayt(a), wa lā muʿṭiya limā manaʿt(a), wa lā yanfa-ʿu dha 'l-jaddi minka 'l-jadd.

There is no god but Allāh, He is One, He has no partner. His is the Sovereignty and His is all praise. He has power over all things. O Allāh, none can withhold that which You bestow and none can bestow that which You withhold and the wealth of the wealthy cannot help them from You [i.e., Your wrath and punishment] (*Bukhārī, Muslim*).[86]

Then also recite:

سُبْحَانَ اللّٰهِ

Subḥān Allāh, Exalted is Allāh

and

اَلْحَمْدُ لِلّٰهِ

Al-ḥamdu li 'Llāh, Praise be to Allāh

thirty three times, then:

اَللّٰهُ أَكْبَرُ

Allāhu akbar, Allāh is the Greatest

thirty four times (*Bukhārī, Muslim*).[87]

8. SPECIAL SUPPLICATION AFTER FAJR AND MAGHRIB

Recite 7 times:

اَللّٰهُمَّ أَجِرْنِيْ مِنَ النَّارِ ۞

Allāhumma ajirnī mina 'n-nār.

O Allāh, save me from the Fire (*Abū Dāwūd*).[88]

9. PRAYER FOR THE NIGHT OF *QADR*

اَللّٰهُمَّ إِنَّكَ عَفُوٌّ تُحِبُّ الْعَفْوَ فَاعْفُ عَنِّيْ ۞

Allāhumma innaka ʿafuwwun tuḥibbu 'l-ʿafwa faʿfu ʿannī.

O Allāh, You are Oft-forgiving, You love
forgiving, so forgive me (*Tirmidhī*).[89]

10. PRAYERS AND SUPPLICATIONS BEFORE SLEEPING

Before retiring to bed, after reciting the *duʿā'* for sleeping (see part 2 above), one should also recite the Verse of the Throne (Āyat al-Kursī) (Qur'ān 2:254), and the final two verses of Sūrat al-Baqara (2:285–286). Thereafter, opening both hands as in *duʿā'*, recite the last three *sūras* of the Holy Qur'ān, and lightly spit on the hands, then pass them over the body thrice, as far as they can reach. Start from the head then proceed to the face, then to the front portion of the body (*Bukhārī*).[90]

Also recite:

أَسْتَغْفِرُ اللّٰهَ الَّذِيْ لَا إِلٰهَ إِلَّا هُوَ الْحَيُّ الْقَيُّوْمُ وَأَتُوْبُ إِلَيْهِ ❁

Astaghfiru 'Llāha 'lladhī lā ilāha illā Huwa
'l-Ḥayyu 'l-Qayyūmu wa atūbu ilayh.

I seek forgiveness from Allāh, Ever-Living and Self- Subsisting,
besides whom there is no god, and I repent to Him.

Whoever recites this *duʿā'*, his sins will be forgiven even if they are as much as the foam of the sea (*Tirmidhī*).[91]

And recite:

سُبْحَانَ اللّٰهِ

Subḥān Allāh, Exalted is Allāh

and

اَلْحَمْدُ لِلّٰهِ

Al-ḥamdu li 'Llāh, Praise be to Allāh

thirty three times, then:

اَللّٰهُ أَكْبَرُ

Allāhu akbar, Allāh is the Greatest

thirty four times (*Bukhārī, Muslim*).[92]

Part 5

أسماء الله الحسنى

The Ninety-Nine Beautiful Names of Allāh

The Messenger of Allāh ﷺ is reported to have said, "There are ninety-nine names of Allāh, whosoever learns them and recites them will certainly enter Paradise" (*Bukhārī*).[93]

They are:

هُوَ اللّٰهُ الَّذِيْ لَآ إِلٰهَ إِلَّا هُوَ. . .

Huwa 'Llāhu 'lladhī lā ilāha illā huw(a)...

He is Allāh besides whom there is no god. He is...

1	The Most Beneficent	Ar-Raḥmān(u)	اَلرَّحْمٰنُ
2	The Most Merciful	Ar-Raḥīm(u)	اَلرَّحِيْمُ
3	The Sovereign	Al-Malik(u)	اَلْمَلِكُ
4	Free From All Blemishes	Al-Quddūs(u)	اَلْقُدُّوْسُ
5	The Giver of Peace/Free From All Blemishes	As-Salām(u)	اَلسَّلَامُ
6	The Guardian of Faith	Al-Mu'min(u)	اَلْمُؤْمِنُ
7	The Protector	Al-Muhaymin(u)	اَلْمُهَيْمِنُ
8	The Mighty	Al-ʿAzīz(u)	اَلْعَزِيْزُ
9	The Overpowering Lord	Al-Jabbār(u)	اَلْجَبَّارُ
10	The Self-Glorifying	Al-Mutakabbir(u)	اَلْمُتَكَبِّرُ

11	The Creator	Al-Khāliq(u)	اَلْخَالِقُ
12	The Evolver	Al-Bāri'(u)	اَلْبَارِئُ
13	The Fashioner	Al-Muṣawwir(u)	اَلْمُصَوِّرُ
14	The Most Forgiving	Al-Ghaffār(u)	اَلْغَفَّارُ
15	The One Who Has Control Over All Things	Al-Qahhār(u)	اَلْقَهَّارُ
16	The Giver of All Things	Al-Wahhāb(u)	اَلْوَهَّابُ
17	The Sustainer and Provider	Ar-Razzāq(u)	اَلرَّزَّاقُ
18	The Remover of Difficulties and Maker of Decisions	Al-Fattāḥ(u)	اَلْفَتَّاحُ
19	The All Knowing	Al-ᶜĀlīm(u)	اَلْعَلِيْمُ
20	The Constrictor	Al-Qābiḍ(u)	اَلْقَابِضُ
21	The Extender of Provisions	Al-Bāsiṭ(u)	اَلْبَاسِطُ
22	The One Who Humbles or Abases	Al-Khāfiḍ(u)	اَلْخَافِضُ
23	The Exalter	Ar-Rāfiᶜ(u)	اَلرَّافِعُ
24	The Giver of Honor	Al-Muᶜizz(u)	اَلْمُعِزُّ
25	The Giver of Disgrace	Al-Mudhill(u)	اَلْمُذِلُّ

26	The All-Hearing	As-Samīʿ(u)	اَلسَّمِيْعُ
27	The All-Seeing	Al-Baṣīr(u)	اَلْبَصِيْرُ
28	The Maker of Immutable Judgments	Al-Ḥakam(u)	اَلْحَكَمُ
29	The Just	Al-ʿAdl(u)	اَلْعَدْلُ
30	The Knower of Innermost Secrets/Benevolent	Al-Laṭīf(u)	اَللَّطِيْفُ
31	The Totally Aware	Al-Khabīr(u)	اَلْخَبِيْرُ
32	The Clement	Al-Ḥalīm(u)	اَلْحَلِيْمُ
33	The Magnificent	Al-ʿAẓīm(u)	اَلْعَظِيْمُ
34	The All-Forgiving	Al-Ghafūr(u)	اَلْغَفُوْرُ
35	The Grateful/One Who Accepts Gratitude	Ash-Shakūr(u)	اَلشَّكُوْرُ
36	The High	Al-ʿAliyy(u)	اَلْعَلِيُّ
37	The Great	Al-Kabīr(u)	اَلْكَبِيْرُ
38	The Protector	Al-Ḥafīẓ(u)	اَلْحَفِيْظُ
39	The Controller of all Things	Al-Muqīt(u)	اَلْمُقِيْتُ
40	The Reckoner/One Who Suffices for Everything	Al-Ḥasīb(u)	اَلْحَسِيْبُ

41	The Majestic	Al-Jalīl(u)	اَلْجَلِيْلُ
42	The Benevolent	Al-Karīm(u)	اَلْكَرِيْمُ
43	The Watchful	Al-Raqīb(u)	اَلرَّقِيْبُ
44	The One Who Responds to Supplication	Al-Mujīb(u)	اَلْمُجِيْبُ
45	The Amply Giving	Al-Wāsiᶜ(u)	اَلْوَاسِعُ
46	The Wise	Al-Ḥakīm(u)	اَلْحَكِيْمُ
47	The Most Loving	Al-Wadūd(u)	اَلْوَدُوْدُ
48	The Most Venerable	Al-Majīd(u)	اَلْمَجِيْدُ
49	The One Who Resurrects	Al-Bāᶜith(u)	اَلْبَاعِثُ
50	The Omnipresent	Ash-Shahīd(u)	اَلشَّهِيْدُ
51	The True	Al-Ḥaqq(u)	اَلْحَقُّ
52	The Guardian	Al-Wakīl(u)	اَلْوَكِيْلُ
53	The Powerful	Al-Qawiyy(u)	اَلْقَوِيُّ
54	The Firm	Al-Matīn(u)	اَلْمَتِيْنُ
55	The Patron	Al-Waliyy(u)	اَلْوَلِيُّ

56	The Praiseworthy	Al-Ḥamīd(u)	اَلْحَمِيْدُ
57	The One Who Records	Al-Muḥṣī	اَلْمُحْصِيْ
58	The Originator	Al-Mubdi'(u)	اَلْمُبْدِئُ
59	The Restorer/Recreator	Al-Muʿīd(u)	اَلْمُعِيْدُ
60	The Giver of Life	Al-Muḥyī	اَلْمُحْيِيْ
61	The Giver of Death	Al-Mumīt(u)	اَلْمُمِيْتُ
62	The Ever-Living	Al-Ḥayy(u)	اَلْحَيُّ
63	The Self-Subsistent	Al-Qayyūm(u)	اَلْقَيُّوْمُ
64	The Inventor	Al-Wājid(u)	اَلْوَاجِدُ
65	The One With Excellence and Veneration	Al-Mājid(u)	اَلْمَاجِدُ
66	The One Unequalled	Al-Wāḥid(u)	اَلْوَاحِدُ
67	The Only	Al-Aḥad(u)	اَلْأَحَدُ
68	The One Free From Want	Aṣ-Ṣamad(u)	اَلصَّمَدُ
69	The One With Authority	Al-Qādir(u)	اَلْقَادِرُ
70	The One With Full Authority	Al-Muqtadir(u)	اَلْمُقْتَدِرُ

71	The Promoter	Al-Muqaddim(u)	اَلْمُقَدِّمُ
72	The Postponer	Al-Mu'akhkhir(u)	اَلْمُؤَخِّرُ
73	The First	Al-Awwal(u)	اَلْأَوَّلُ
74	The Last	Al-Ākhir(u)	اَلْآخِرُ
75	The Manifest	Aẓ-Ẓāhir(u)	اَلظَّاهِرُ
76	The Hidden	Al-Bāṭin(u)	اَلْبَاطِنُ
77	The One Who Exercises Power Over All	Al-Wālī	اَلْوَالِيْ
78	The One Far Above the Creation	Al-Muta-ʿālī	اَلْمُتَعَالِيْ
79	The One Who Treats With Kindness	Al-Barr(u)	اَلْبَرُّ
80	The Ever Relenting	Al-Tawwāb(u)	اَلتَّوَّابُ
81	The Avenger	Al-Muntaqim(u)	اَلْمُنْتَقِمُ
82	The Pardoner	Al-ʿAfuww(u)	اَلْعَفُوُّ
83	The Affectionate	Ar-Ra'ūf(u)	اَلرَّؤُوْفُ
84	The Possessor of Sovereignty	Māliku 'l-mulk(i)	مَالِكُ الْمُلْكِ
85	The Lord of Majesty and Benevolence	Dhū 'l-jalāli wa 'l-ikrām(i)	ذُو الْجَلَالِ وَالْإِكْرَامِ

86	The Just	Al-Muqsiṭ(u)	اَلْمُقْسِطُ
87	The Assembler	Al-Jāmiᶜ(u)	اَلْجَامِعُ
88	The Free From Want	Al-Ghaniyy(u)	اَلْغَنِيُّ
89	The Enricher	Al-Mughnī	اَلْمُغْنِيْ
90	The One Who Prohibits	Al-Māniᶜ(u)	اَلْمَانِعُ
91	The One Who Brings Distress	Aḍ-Ḍārr(u)	اَلضَّارُّ
92	The Benefactor	An-Nāfiᶜ(u)	اَلنَّافِعُ
93	The Light	An-Nūr(u)	اَلنُّوْرُ
94	The Guide	Al-Hādī	اَلْهَادِيْ
95	The Deviser	Al-Badīᶜ(u)	اَلْبَدِيْعُ
96	The Eternal	Al-Bāqī	اَلْبَاقِيْ
97	The Supporter/The Inheritor	Al-Wārith(u)	اَلْوَارِثُ
98	The One Who Loves Virtue or Guidance Toward Virtue	Ar-Rashīd(u)	اَلرَّشِيْدُ
99	The Most Forbearing	Aṣ-Ṣabūr(u)	اَلصَّبُوْرُ

(*Tirmidhī*).

Part 6

صيغ الصلاة والسلام

على النبي

صلى الله عليه وسلم

Blessings & Salutations on the Prophet ﷺ

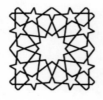

اَللّٰهُمَّ صَلِّ عَلٰى مُحَمَّدٍ وَّعَلٰى آلِ مُحَمَّدٍ كَمَا صَلَّيْتَ عَلٰى إِبْرَاهِيْمَ وَعَلٰى
آلِ إِبْرَاهِيْمَ إِنَّكَ حَمِيْدٌ مَّجِيْدٌ. اَللّٰهُمَّ بَارِكْ عَلٰى مُحَمَّدٍ وَّعَلٰى آلِ مُحَمَّدٍ
كَمَا بَارَكْتَ عَلٰى إِبْرَاهِيْمَ وَعَلٰى آلِ إِبْرَاهِيْمَ إِنَّكَ حَمِيْدٌ مَّجِيْدٌ

Allāhumma ṣalli ʿalā Muḥammadiw wa ʿalā āli Muḥammadin kamā ṣallayta ʿalā Ibrāhīma wa ʿalā āli Ibrāhīma innaka ḥamīdum majīd(un). Allāhumma bārik ʿalā Muḥammadiw wa ʿalā āli Muḥammadin kamā bārakta ʿalā Ibrāhīma wa ʿalā āli Ibrāhīma innaka ḥamidum majīd.

O Allāh, send Your mercy on Muḥammad and on his descendants as You have sent Your mercy on Ibrāhīm and his descendants. Verily, You are the Great and Praiseworthy. O Allāh, send Your blessings on Muḥammad and on his descendants, as You have sent Your blessings on Ibrāhīm and his descendants. Verily, You are Great and Praiseworthy (*Bukhārī*).[94]

These are the salutations (*ṣalawāt*) that are read in prayer.

اَللّٰهُمَّ صَلِّ عَلٰى مُحَمَّدِنِ النَّبِيِّ الْأُمِّيِّ وَعَلٰى آلِهٖ وَسَلِّمْ تَسْلِيْمًا

Allāhumma ṣalli ʿalā Muḥammadini ʼn-nabiyyi ʼl-ummiyyi wa ʿalā ālihī wa sallim taslīmā.

O Allāh send Your mercy on the Unlettered Prophet Muḥammad and on his family and shower him with peace.

Whoever recites this 80 times on Friday after the ʿAṣr prayer before moving from his place, 80 years of his sins will be forgiven and 80 years of worship will be allocated to him (*Jāmiʿ al-Ṣaghīr, Al-Qawl al-Badīʿ*).[95]

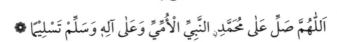

جَزَى اللّٰهُ عَنَّا مُحَمَّدًا صَلَّى اللّٰهُ عَلَيْهِ وَسَلَّمَ مَا هُوَ أَهْلُهُ ۞

Jaza 'Llāhu ʿannā Muḥammadan ṣalla 'Llāhu ʿalayhi wa sallama mā huwa ahluh.

Allāh reward Muḥammad ﷺ on behalf of us with what he is worthy of.

Whoever recites this prayer, 70 angels will be given the task of writing virtues for him for a thousand days (*Ṭabarānī*).[96]

~

اَللّٰهُمَّ صَلِّ عَلٰى مُحَمَّدٍ عَبْدِكَ وَرَسُوْلِكَ وَصَلِّ عَلَى الْمُؤْمِنِيْنَ وَالْمُؤْمِنَاتِ وَالْمُسْلِمِيْنَ وَالْمُسْلِمَاتِ ۞

Allāhumma ṣalli ʿalā Muḥammadin ʿabdika wa rasūlika wa ṣalli ʿala 'l-mu'minīna wa 'l-mu'mināt(i) wa 'l-muslimīna wa 'l-muslimāt.

O Allāh send Your mercy on Muḥammad, Your servant, Your Messenger and send mercy on all believing men and women and all Muslim men and women (*Ibn Ḥibbān*).[97]

~

اَللّٰهُمَّ صَلِّ عَلٰى مُحَمَّدٍ وَّعَلٰى آلِ مُحَمَّدٍ، وَّأَنْزِلْهُ الْمَقْعَدَ الْمُقَرَّبَ عِنْدَكَ يَوْمَ الْقِيَامَةِ ۞

Allāhumma ṣalli ʿalā Muḥammadiw wa ʿalā āli Muḥammad(iw), wa anzilhu 'l-maqʿada 'l-muqarraba ʿindaka yawma 'l-qiyāmah.

O Allāh send Your mercy on Muḥammad and on the family of

Muḥammad and appoint him a blessed place close to You on the Day of Judgment (*Ṭabarānī*).[98]

اَللّٰهُمَّ صَلِّ عَلٰى مُحَمَّدِنِ النَّبِيِّ وَأَزْوَاجِهٖ أُمَّهَاتِ الْمُؤْمِنِيْنَ وَذُرِّيَّتِهٖ وَأَهْلِ بَيْتِهٖ ۞

Allāhumma ṣallī ʿalā Muḥammadini 'n-nabiyyi wa azwājihī ummahāti 'l-mu'minīna wa dhurriyyatihī wa ahli baytih.

O Allāh, send Your blessings on Muḥammad, on his wives, the mothers of the believers, on his descendants and on his family (*Abū Dāwūd*).[99]

اَللّٰهُمَّ اجْعَلْ صَلَوَاتِكَ وَرَحْمَتَكَ وَبَرَكَاتِكَ عَلٰى مُحَمَّدٍ وَّعَلٰى آلِ مُحَمَّدٍ كَمَا جَعَلْتَهَا عَلٰى آلِ إِبْرَاهِيْمَ ۞

Allāhumma 'jʿal ṣalawātika wa raḥmataka wa barakātika ʿalā Muḥammadiw wa ʿalā āli Muḥammadin kamā ja-ʿaltahā ʿalā āli Ibrāhīm.

O Allāh, shower Your salutations, Your mercy, and Your blessings upon Muḥammad and the family of Muḥammad as You did upon the family of Ibrāhīm (*Aḥmad*).[100]

Part 7

فضائل بعض السور والآيات

Virtues of Various Chapters & Verses of the Holy Qur'ān

The Excellence of Sūrat al-Fātiḥa

There is cure for every disease in Sūrat al-Fātiḥa (*Dārimī*).[101]

Sūrat al-Fātiḥa is the greatest and most virtuous sūra of the Holy Qur'ān (*Abū Dāwūd, Ibn Māja*).[102]

Once while Jibrīl ﷷ was seated with the Messenger of Allāh ﷺ, he suddenly heard a sound of something cracking from above. Jibrīl ﷷ lifted his head and said, "This is a door of Heaven being opened, which has never been opened before. This is an angel descending to the earth and never before did he descend." The angel came to the Prophet ﷺ, and said, "Be pleased with two lights which no other Prophet before you has been given: the Opening [chapter] of the Book (Fātiḥat al-Kitāb); and the closing two verses (*khawātīm*) of Sūrat al-Baqara. You will not recite even one letter of these verses without being given a reward for it" (*Muslim*).[103]

The Excellence of Āyat al-Kursī

Āyat al-Kursī is the greatest verse of the Holy Qur'ān (*Muslim*).[104]

It is the leader of the verses of the Holy Qur'ān (*Tirmidhī*).[105]

The Excellence of the Last Two Verses of Sūrat al-Baqara

Reciting the final two verses of this *sūra* will protect [the reciter] from anything undesirable happening in the night [i.e., it will be a safeguard from the Satan, burglars, etc.] (*Muslim*).[106]

Allāh has completed Sūrat al-Baqara with two such verses that have been given to me from the treasures kept beneath the Throne, so learn them and teach them to your wives and children for they are a source of mercy, a form of recitation, and are prayers (*Mustadrak*).[107]

The Excellence of Sūrat al-Kahf

For the person who recites it on the eve of Friday [the night between Thursday and Friday], it will provide [for him] a light (*nūr*) from one Friday to the next (*Mustadrak*).[108]

Whoever recites the last ten verses of Sūrat al-Kahf, and then Dajjāl, "the Anti-Christ," reveals himself [during the reciter's life time], he will have no influence on the reciter (*Ṭabarānī*).[109]

Whoever commits to memory the first ten verses of Sūrat al-Kahf, will be safeguarded from the mischief of Dajjāl (*Muslim*).[110]

The Excellence of Sūra Yāsīn

Recite Sūra Yāsīn [morning and evening] especially when in the presence of someone dying or after he has died, for it is mentioned in a ḥadīth that Sūra Yāsīn is the heart of the Qur'ān, and anyone who recites it for the pleasure of Allāh and seeking [reward of the] Hereafter, Allāh will forgive him. It is also related, "Recite it in the presence of a dying person" (*Abū Dāwūd, Nasā'ī*).[111]

A ḥadīth states, "Whoever recites Yāsīn in the beginning of the day all his needs are fulfilled" (*Daylamī*).[112]

The Excellence of Sūrat al-Mulk

The Messenger of Allāh ﷺ said, "It is my desire that Sūrat al-Mulk should be in the heart of every Believer" (*Muslim*).[113]

According to another ḥadīth the Messenger of Allāh ﷺ said, "A *sūra* in the Qur'ān consisting of thirty verses will intercede on behalf of its reciter until he is forgiven: "*Tabāraka 'lladhī bi yadihi 'l-mulk* [Sūrat al-Mulk]" (*Abū Dāwūd, Tirmidhī, Nasā'ī*). Another narration states that "it will argue on behalf of its reciter until it enters him into Paradise" (*Ṭabarānī*).

The Excellence of Sūrat al-Ikhlāṣ

The Messenger of Allāh ﷺ said, "I swear by the One in whose hand is my life that Sūrat al-Ikhlāṣ is equivalent to a third of the Qur'ān" (*Bukhārī*).[114]

It is mentioned in a ḥadīth that a certain Companion always used to recite Sūrat al-Ikhlāṣ together with other *sūras* in every *rakʿa* of prayer he used to perform. On being asked the reason, he replied that he loved this *sūra* very much. When the Messenger of Allāh ﷺ heard this, he said, "The love for this *sūra* will admit you into Paradise" (*Tirmidhī*).[115]

The Excellence of Sūrat al-Falaq & Sūrat al-Nās

The Messenger of Allāh ﷺ used to invoke Allāh's protection against the mischief of Jinn and the evil eye of men [using various words], until Allāh revealed the *Muʿawwadhatayn* (Sūrat al-Falaq and Sūrat al-Nās) to him. So he held firmly to these and discarded all others (*Tirmidhī*).[116]

A ḥadīth states, "No one ever asked [of Allāh] with the like of these *sūras* and no one ever sought refuge [in Allāh] with the like of these two *sūras*" (*Nasā'ī*).[117]

Part 8

الصلوات النافلة

Optional Prayers

Taḥiyyat al-Wuḍū' (Greeting of the Ablution)

It is recommended to perform two *rakʿas* after ablution (*wuḍū'*). The Messenger of Allāh ﷺ said, "He who observes two *rakʿas* with full devotion after performing *wuḍū'* well, becomes entitled to enter Paradise" (*Muslim*).[118]

Taḥiyyat al-Masjid (Greeting of the Masjid)

It is recommended to perform two *rakʿas* (or more) upon entry into the *masjid*, before sitting down, as a greeting to the *masjid*. The Messenger of Allāh ﷺ said, "When one of you enters the *masjid*, he should not sit down until he has offered two *rakʿas*" (*Bukhārī, Muslim*).[119] If the *farḍ* prayer is in progress when one enters, one should not perform the *Taḥiyyat al-Masjid*—the *farḍ* prayer will suffice, and the person will receive the reward of the *Taḥiyyat al-Masjid*. Although one should perform this prayer prior to sitting down, if one happens to sit down, he may still perform the prayer but its reward is less. It is sufficient for a person who frequents the *masjid* several times a day, to perform the prayer once, but preferable to perform it each time. However, one should avoid performing it during the disliked (*makrūh*) times (see Prayer for Repentance below).

Ṣalāt al-Ishrāq (Sunrise Prayer)

It is recommended to perform two to four *rakʿas* approximately twenty minutes after sunrise in the same place that one has performed his Fajr prayer. The Messenger of Allāh ﷺ said, "The person who performs two *rakʿas* of *Ishrāq* prayer has all his sins forgiven; if he dies the same day, he will be admitted to Paradise" (*Ṭabarānī*).[120]

Following the Fajr prayer one remains seated in his place, busy in the remembrance of Allāh (*dhikr*), sending blessings on the Messenger of Allāh ﷺ, making remembrance of Allāh, reciting the Qur'ān, or listening to a religious talk, etc. Then one performs the *Ishrāq* prayer when its time sets in. One can still perform it even after one has indulged in worldly affairs although the reward will be less.

ṢALĀT AL-ḌUḤĀ (LATE MORNING PRAYER)

It is recommended to perform two to twelve *rakʿas* in units of two after some portion of the morning has passed (around 10 AM) until noon (when the sun reaches its zenith at midday). Muʿādha al-ʿAdawiyya 🌼 narrates that once she enquired from ʿĀʾisha 🌼 regarding how many *rakʿas* of prayer the Messenger of Allāh 🌸 performed for the Ḍuḥā prayer. She replied, "Four *rakʿas* and thereafter as many as Allāh willed" (*Muslim*).[121] Anas 🌼 narrates that the Messenger of Allāh 🌸 said, "Whoever performs twelve *rakʿas* for the Ḍuḥā prayer, Allāh will build for him a castle of gold in Paradise" (*Tirmidhī*).[122] Abū Hurayra 🌼 narrates that the Messenger of Allāh 🌸 said, "Whoever is particular in performing two *rakʿas* of prayer at noon, all his sins will be forgiven, even though they may be as much as the foam of the ocean" (*Tirmidhī, Ibn Māja*).[123]

According to many scholars, both the *Ishrāq* and Ḍuḥā prayers are one and the same prayer, its time extending from after sunrise to just before noon.

ṢALĀT AL-AWWĀBĪN (PRAYER OF THE PIOUS)

It is recommended to perform anywhere between six to twenty *rakʿas* following the Maghrib prayer, preferably in two *rakʿa* units, otherwise four. ʿAmmār ibn Yāsir 🌼 narrates that the Messenger of Allāh 🌸 performed six *rakʿas* after Maghrib and said, "Whosoever offers six *rakʿas* after the Maghrib prayer, will have all his sins forgiven even if they are as much as the foam of the ocean" (*Ṭabarānī*).[124] Abū Hurayra 🌼 narrates that the Messenger of Allāh 🌸 said, "Whoever performs six *rakʿas* after the Maghrib prayer and does not speak any evil between them, then the six [*rakʿas*] will be equal to the reward of twelve years of worship" (*Tirmidhī, Ibn Māja*).[125] Some scholars consider that the two *rakʿas* of emphasized (*mu'akkada*) *sunna* prayer after Maghrib suffices for two *rakʿas* of *Awwābīn* prayer, hence, a person may perform another four to complete the minimum six *rakʿas*.

Ṣalāt al-Tawba (Prayer for Repentance)

It is recommended to perform two or more *rakʿas* before one makes repentance. This prayer can be performed at any time except at the offensive (*makrūh*) times, which are as follows: following the Fajr prayer until after sunrise, after ʿAṣr prayer until after sunset, and when the sun is at its zenith. ʿAlī ﷺ narrates that Abū Bakr ﷺ related to him that he heard the Messenger of Allāh ﷺ say, "Whoever commits a sin, and then gets up and performs ablution, then offers prayers seeking the forgiveness of Allāh, Allāh will certainly forgive him." After this the Prophet ﷺ recited the following verse of the Qur'ān: "And those who, having done an act of indecency or wronged their own selves, remember Allāh and ask for forgiveness for their sins, and who can forgive sins except Allāh? And those who are never obstinate in persisting knowingly in [the wrong] they have done" (Qur'ān 3:135) (*Tirmidhī*).[126] After performing these two *rakʿas*, a person should raise his hands with sincerity and humility and repent abundantly. By the grace of Allāh, he will be forgiven.

Ṣalāt al-Istikhāra (Prayer for Decision Making)

When one needs to make decisions in life or needs blessings in something one is undertaking, for instance, marriage, buying property, starting a business, making a journey, or any other matter, he should perform two *rakʿas* of prayer and, thereafter, recite the following *duʿā'*:

اَللّٰهُمَّ إِنِّيْ أَسْتَخِيْرُكَ بِعِلْمِكَ وَاَسْتَقْدِرُكَ بِقُدْرَتِكَ وَأَسْأَلُكَ مِنْ فَضْلِكَ الْعَظِيْمِ، فَإِنَّكَ تَقْدِرُ وَلَا أَقْدِرُ وَتَعْلَمُ وَلَا أَعْلَمُ وَأَنْتَ عَلَّامُ الْغُيُوْبِ، اَللّٰهُمَّ إِنْ كُنْتَ تَعْلَمُ أَنَّ [هٰذَا الْأَمْرَ] خَيْرٌ لِّيْ فِيْ دِيْنِيْ وَمَعَاشِيْ وَعَاقِبَةِ أَمْرِيْ، فَاقْدِرْهُ لِيْ وَيَسِّرْهُ لِيْ ثُمَّ بَارِكْ لِيْ فِيْهِ، وَإِنْ كُنْتَ تَعْلَمُ أَنَّ [هٰذَا الْأَمْرَ] شَرٌّ لِّيْ فِيْ دِيْنِيْ وَمَعَاشِيْ وَعَاقِبَةِ أَمْرِيْ، فَاصْرِفْهُ عَنِّيْ وَاصْرِفْنِيْ عَنْهُ، وَاقْدِرْ لِيَ الْخَيْرَ حَيْثُ كَانَ، ثُمَّ أَرْضِنِيْ بِهٖ ۞

Allāḥumma innī astakhīruka bi ʿilmika wa astaqdiruka bi qudratika wa as'aluka min faḍlika 'l-ʿaẓīm(i), fa innaka taqdiru wa lā aqdiru wa taʿlamu wa lā aʿlamu wa Anta ʿAllāmu 'l-ghuyūb(i), Allāhumma in kunta taʿlamu anna [hādha 'l-amra] khayrul lī fī dīnī wa ma-ʿashī wa ʿāqibati amrī, fa 'qdirhu lī wa yassirhu lī thumma bārik lī fīḥ(i), wa in kunta taʿlamu anna [hādha 'l-amra] sharrul lī fī dīnī wa ma-ʿāshī wa ʿāqibati amrī, fa 'ṣrifhu ʿannī wa 'ṣrifnī ʿanhu wa 'qdir liya 'l-khayra ḥaythu kān(a), thumma arḍinī bih.

O Allāh, I ask of You the good through Your knowledge and I ask You to grant me ability through Your power and beg Your favor of infinite bounty, for surely, You have power and I have none, You know all and I know nothing, and You are the Knower of all that is hidden. O Allāh if, in Your knowledge, *this matter* be good for my faith, my livelihood and the outcome of my affairs in the world and the Hereafter, then ordain it for me and facilitate it for me and grant me blessing in it. But, if in Your knowledge *this matter* is bad for my faith, my livelihood and the outcome of my affairs in the world and the Hereafter, then turn it away from me and turn me away from it, and ordain for me the good wherever it be, and cause me to be pleased with it (*Bukhārī*).[127]

When one reaches the words أَنَّ هٰذَا الأَمْرَ (anna hādha 'l-amra) "this matter," one should think about the matter one is seeking a decision on or blessings for. After that, scholars state that one should sleep in a state of purity on a clean bed, with one's face toward the *qibla*. Whatever comes to mind upon waking will be the best course of action and should be adopted. If no resolution comes to mind on the first day and the anxiety and indecisiveness continues, one should repeat it the next day and so on for a week (otherwise until a decision comes to mind). By the grace of Allāh one will come to know the good or detriment of the matter. One must remember that it is not necessary that a person see a dream relating to his matter. One of the benefits of this *duʿā'* is that it can also help one overcome emotional attachments.

Short Prayer for Seeking Divine Help & Guidance

اَللّٰهُمَّ خِرْ لِيْ وَاخْتَرْ لِيْ ۞

Allāḥumma khir lī wa 'khtar lī.

O Allāh, choose and select for me [the better of the two] (*Tirmidhī*).[128]

This *duʿā'* is very useful for on the spot decisions that one may need to make.

Ṣalāt al-Ḥāja (Prayer for Need)

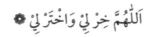

It is recommended to perform two or more *rakʿas* when one is in need or in difficulty. The Messenger of Allāh ﷺ said, "Whoever is in need of something, should make a perfect ablution [i.e., by observing all its rules and etiquette] and perform two *rakʿas* of prayer. After it, he should praise Allāh, send blessings on His Messenger ﷺ and then recite the [following] *duʿā'*:

لَا إِلٰهَ إِلَّا اللّٰهُ الْحَلِيْمُ الْكَرِيْمُ، سُبْحَانَ اللّٰهِ رَبِّ الْعَرْشِ الْعَظِيْمِ، اَلْحَمْدُ لِلّٰهِ رَبِّ الْعَالَمِيْنَ، أَسْأَلُكَ مُوْجِبَاتِ رَحْمَتِكَ، وَعَزَائِمَ مَغْفِرَتِكَ، وَالْغَنِيْمَةَ مِنْ كُلِّ بِرٍّ، وَّالسَّلَامَةَ مِنْ كُلِّ إِثْمٍ، لَّا تَدَعْ لِي ذَنْبًا إِلَّا غَفَرْتَهُ، وَلَا هَمًّا إِلَّا فَرَّجْتَهُ، وَلَا حَاجَةً هِيَ لَكَ رِضًا إِلَّا قَضَيْتَهَا يَا أَرْحَمَ الرَّاحِمِيْنَ ۞

Lā ilāha illa 'Llāhu 'l-Ḥalīmu 'l-Karīm(u), subḥāna 'Llāhi Rabbi 'l-ʿarshi 'l-ʿaẓīm(i), al-ḥamdu li 'Llāhi Rabbi 'l-ʿālamīn(a), as'aluka mūjibāti raḥmatik(a), wa ʿazā'ima maghfiratik(a), wa 'l-ghanīmata min kulli birr(iw), wa 's-salāmata min kulli ithm(in), lā tadaʿ lī dhamban illā ghafartah(ū), wa lā hamman illā farrajtah(ū), wa lā ḥājatan hiya laka riḍan illā qaḍaytahā yā Arḥamar rāḥimīn.

There is no god but Allāh, the Most Forbearing and Generous. Exalted is Allāh the Lord of the Great Throne. Praise be to Allāh, the Lord of the worlds. I ask of You those things which will procure Your mercy, and Your immense forgiveness, a full share of virtuous deeds, and complete safety from iniquity. Do not let any sin of mine to be left unforgiven, nor any worry and pain unrelieved, nor any need which is a source of pleasure for You unfulfilled, O Most Merciful of the merciful (*Tirmidhī*).[129]

Thereafter, one should make a passionate *duʿā'* for the fulfillment of one's need or delivery from one's difficulty.

Ṣalāt al-Tasbīḥ (Prayer of Glorification)

ʿAbdullāh ibn ʿAbbās ☙ narrates that the Messenger of Allāh ﷺ said to his uncle ʿAbbās ibn ʿAbd al-Muṭṭalib, "O ʿAbbās! O my respected uncle! May I offer you a precious gift and a valuable present? May I tell you something special? May I do something special? May I perform ten tasks for you and render you ten services (i.e., inform you of an act from which ten benefits may be obtained) [for which] Allāh will forgive all your sins of the past as well as the future, old as well as new, intentional as well as unintentional, major as well as minor, and the hidden as well as the apparent? It is Ṣalāt al-Tasbīḥ.[130]

This prayer consists of four rakʿas and there are two ways in which it may be performed. The following tasbīḥ should be recited a total of three hundred times in the four rakʿas:

$$ \text{❂} \; \text{سُبْحَانَ اللّٰهِ وَالْحَمْدُ لِلّٰهِ وَلَا إِلٰهَ إِلَّا اللّٰهُ وَاللّٰهُ أَكْبَرُ} $$

Subḥāna 'Llāhi wa 'l-ḥamdu li 'Llāhi wa lā ilāha illa 'Llāhu wa 'Llāhu akbar.

Exalted is Allāh, Praise be to Allāh, there is none worthy of worship except Allāh, and Allāh is the Greatest.

Method 1: After reciting Sūra al-Fātiḥa and a sūra in the first rakʿa, remain standing and recite the above tasbīḥ fifteen times. Then go into rukūʿ (bowing) and recite it ten times after the tasbīḥs of rukūʿ. After rukūʿ recite the tasbīḥ ten times in the standing position. In sajda (prostration) recite the tasbīḥ ten times after the tasbīḥs of sajda. In the sitting posture between the two prostrations recite the tasbīḥ ten times. In the second sajda recite the tasbīḥ ten times also. After the second sajda, instead of standing up immediately, remain seated and recite the tasbīḥ ten times. Thereafter stand for the second rakʿa. The same procedure is followed in each of the four rakʿas.

Method 2: In this method, three hundred *tasbīḥs* are also recited. The only difference is that the *tasbīḥ* will be recited fifteen times after the initial *duʿā'* of the prayer (*thanā'*) before Sūrat al-Fātiḥa and then ten times after reciting a *sūra* before *rukūʿ*: this second set of ten will be in place of the ten that are recited after the second prostration of every *rakʿā* (in method 1).

Note: According to the first method, the *tasbīḥ* will be recited ten times before the *tashahhud* in the second and fourth *rakʿas*. According to the second method, the *tasbīḥ* will not be recited before the *tashahhud* in the second and fourth *rakʿas* since it will have already been recited in the initial standing posture. Intention for this prayer is that one is performing four *rakʿas Ṣalāt al-Tasbīḥ*. There are no specific *sūras* to be recited in *Ṣalāt al-Tasbīḥ*. One should not count the number of *tasbīḥs* verbally, since this will invalidate the prayer. One can keep track of how may *tasbīḥs* one has recited by moving the fingers slightly or pressing them down slightly. If the *tasbīḥs* of a particular posture are omitted, then they should be recited in the next posture, e.g. if the *tasbīḥs* before Sūrat al-Fātiḥa are omitted, they should be recited at the end of the recitation, and if the *tasbīḥs* between the two prostrations are omitted they should be recited in the second prostration.

Ṣalāt al-Tahajjud (Night Vigil Prayer)

One of the most virtuous prayer after the *farḍ* prayers is the *Tahajjud* prayer. Its time sets in after one has performed ʿIshā' prayer and remains until Fajr time. However, it is superior to perform this prayer in the final third portion of the night and delay one's *witr* prayer until after it. It is recommended to perform eight *rakʿas* in two or four units followed by three *rakʿas witr*. Allāh says: "Worship him in a portion of the night and glorify him through the night" (Qur'ān 76:26). The Messenger of Allāh ﷺ said, "Make a habit of observing the *Tahajjud* prayer. It was the custom of the pious before you. It draws you close to your Lord, and keeps you away from sins" (*Tirmidhī*).[131] Abū Hurayra ﷺ narrates that he heard the Messenger of Allāh ﷺ say, "The most excellent prayer after the obligatory prayers is the one in the depth of the night" (*Aḥmad*).[132] If one has performed the *witr* prayer and then happens to wake up for *Tahajjud*, there is nothing wrong with him performing the *Tahajjud* and it will not invalidate his *witr* prayer. However, where possible it is superior to delay the *witr* prayer and make it the last prayer that one performs at night.

Ṣalāt al-Safar (Prayer for Travel)

It is recommended to perform two *rakʿas* of *nafl* (supererogatory) prayer before setting out on a journey and likewise upon returning.

REFERENCES

1 أخرجه البخاري في : كتاب الوضوء
2 أخرجه البخاري في : كتاب الوضوء ومسلم في كتاب الذكر والدعاء
3 أخرجه البخاري في : كتاب الدعوات ومسلم في الذكر والدعاء
4 أخرجه الترمذي في : أبواب الطهارة
5 أخرجه البخاري في : كتاب الوضوء ومسلم في : كتاب الحيض
6 أخرجه الترمذي في : أبواب الطهارة وأبو داؤد في : كتاب الطهارة
7 أخرجه ابن السني
8 أخرجه مسلم في : كتاب الطهارة
9 أخرجه الترمذي في : أبواب الطهارة والنسائي في : كتاب الطهارة
10 أخرجه البخاري في : كتاب الأذان
11 أخرجه مسلم في : كتاب صلاة المسافر
12 أخرجه مسلم في : كتاب صلاة المسافر
13 أخرجه الحاكم في المستدرك في : كتاب الأطعمة
14 أخرجه الترمذي في : أبواب الدعوات وأبو داؤد في : كتاب الأطعمة
15 أخرجه الترمذي في : أبواب الدعوات وأبو داؤد في كتاب اللباس
16 أخرجه أبو داؤد في : كتاب الأطعمة
17 أخرجه ابن ماجة في : كتاب الصوم
18 أخرجه أبو داؤد في المراسيل
19 أخرجه مسلم في : كتاب الأطعمة
20 أخرجه الترمذي في : أبواب الدعوات
21 أخرجه الحاكم في المستدرك في : كتاب الدعاء
22 أخرجه الترمذي في : أبواب الدعوات وأبو داؤد في كتاب اللباس
23 أخرجه الترمذي في : أبواب الدعوات
24 أخرجه ابن السني
25 أخرجه ابن ماجة
26 أخرجه الترمذي في : أبواب الدعوات وأبو داؤد في كتاب الأدب
27 أخرجه الترمذي في : أبواب الدعوات وأبو داؤد في كتاب الأدب
28 أخرجه أبو داؤد في كتاب الأدب
29 أخرجه ابن السني
30 أخرجه مسلم في : كتاب الذكر والدعاء والترمذي في : أبواب الدعوات وأبو داؤد في كتاب الأدب
31 أخرجه أبو داؤد في كتاب الأدب

32 أخرجه الترمذي في : أبواب الدعوات
33 أخرجه الترمذي في : أبواب الدعوات وأبو داؤد في كتاب الجهاد
34 أخرجه الترمذي في : أبواب الدعوات
35 أخرجه البخاري في : كتاب الحج
36 أخرجه الترمذي في : أبواب الدعوات وأخرجه الحاكم في المستدرك في : كتاب الدعاء
37 أخرجه البخاري في : كتاب الأدب
38 أخرجه الترمذي في : أبواب الدعوات
39 أخرجه البخاري في : كتاب بدء الخلق وأبو داؤد في كتاب الأدب
40 أخرجه الترمذي في : أبواب الدعوات والحاكم في المستدرك في : كتاب الدعاء
41 أخرجه الحاكم في المستدرك في : كتاب الدعاء
42 أخرجه ابن السني
43 أخرجه أبو داؤد في كتاب الأدب
44 أخرجه الترمذي في : أبواب الدعوات
45 أخرجه أبو داؤد في كتاب الصلاة
46 أخرجه مسلم في : كتاب الطب
47 أخرجه أبو داؤد في كتاب الأقضية
48 أخرجه البخاري في : كتاب الدعوات ومسلم في : كتاب الذكر والدعاء
49 أخرجه الحاكم في المستدرك في : كتاب الدعاء
50 أخرجه الترمذي في : أبواب الدعوات
51 أخرجه الحاكم في المستدرك في : كتاب الدعاء
52 أخرجه الحاكم في المستدرك في : كتاب الدعاء
53 أخرجه البخاري في : كتاب الأدب ومسلم في : كتاب البر والصلة والتقوى
54 أخرجه ابن السني
55 أخرجه الترمذي في : أبواب الدعوات ومالك في المؤطا في : كتاب الجامع
56 أخرجه مالك في المؤطا في : كتاب الجامع
57 أخرجه البخاري في : كتاب الطب
58 أخرجه البخاري في : كتاب الطب
59 أخرجه ابن السني
60 أخرجه الترمذي في : أبواب الدعوات
61 أخرجه مالك في المؤطا في : كتاب النكاح والترمذي في : أبواب الدعوات
62 أخرجه البخاري في : كتاب الدعوات
63 أخرجه البخاري في : كتاب الجنائز تعليقًا عن حسن البصرى ووصله عبد الرزاق في مصنفه
64 أخرجه الترمذي في : أبواب الجنائز
65 أخرجه مسلم في : كتاب الإيمان
66 أخرجه مسلم في : كتاب الإيمان
67 أخرجه البخاري في : كتاب الحج

68 أخرجه مسلم في : كتاب الذكر والدعاء
69 أخرجه مسلم في : كتاب الذكر والدعاء
70 أخرجه الحاكم في المستدرك في : كتاب الدعاء والترمذي في أبواب الدعوات
71 أخرجه البخاري في : كتاب تفسير القرآن ومسلم في : كتاب الذكر والدعاء
72 أخرجه البخاري في : كتاب الدعوات ومسلم في : كتاب الذكر والدعاء
73 أخرجه الترمذي في أبواب الدعوات
74 أخرجه الحاكم في المستدرك في : كتاب الدعاء
75 أخرجه الحاكم في المستدرك في : كتاب الدعاء
76 أخرجه الترمذي في أبواب الدعوات
77 أخرجه الترمذي في أبواب الدعوات
78 أخرجه البخاري في : كتاب الدعوات
79 أخرجه أبو داؤد في : كتاب الصلاة والترمذي في : أبواب الصلاة والنسائي في : قيام الليل
80 أخرجه عبد الرزاق في مصنفه في : باب القنوت
81 أخرجه ابن أبي شيبة في المصنف في : باب في قنوت الوتر وما يقرأ فيه
82 أخرجه النسائي في : باب الوتر
83 أخرجه أبو داؤد في : كتاب الصلاة
84 أخرجه البخاري في : كتاب الدعوات
85 أخرجه مسلم في : باب الذكر بعد الصلاة
86 أخرجه البخاري في : كتاب الدعوات ومسلم في : باب الذكر بعد الصلاة
87 أخرجه البخاري في : كتاب الدعوات ومسلم في : باب الذكر بعد الصلاة
88 أخرجه أبو داؤد في : كتاب الادب
89 أخرجه الترمذي في : أبواب الدعوات
90 أخرجه البخاري في : كتاب الدعوات
91 أخرجه الترمذي في : أبواب الدعوات
92 أخرجه البخاري في : كتاب الدعوات ومسلم في : باب الذكر بعد الصلاة
93 أخرجه البخاري في : كتاب الدعوات
94 أخرجه البخاري في : كتاب الدعوات
95 أخرجه السخاوي في القول البديع في الصلاة على الحبيب الشفيع والسيوطي في الجامع الصغير
96 أخرجه الطبراني
97 أخرجه ابن حبان
98 أخرجه الطبراني في الكبير والأوسط
99 أخرجه أبو داؤد
100 أخرجه أحمد
101 أخرجه الدارمي في كتاب فضائل القرآن
102 أخرجه أبو داؤد وابن ماجة
103 أخرجه مسلم في : كتاب فضائل القرآن

104 أخرجه مسلم في : كتاب فضائل القرآن
105 أخرجه الترمذي في : أبواب فضائل القرآن
106 أخرجه مسلم في : كتاب فضائل القرآن
107 أخرجه الحاكم في مستدركه في : كتاب فضائل القرآن
108 أخرجه الحاكم في مستدركه في : كتاب فضائل القرآن
109 أخرجه الطبراني في الأوسط
110 أخرجه مسلم في : كتاب فضائل القرآن
111 أخرجه النسائي وأبو داؤد
112 أخرجه الديلمي
113 أخرجه مسلم في : كتاب فضائل القرآن
114 أخرجه البخاري
115 أخرجه الترمذي في : أبواب فضائل القرآن
116 أخرجه الترمذي في : أبواب فضائل القرآن
117 أخرجه النسائي
118 أخرجه مسلم في : كتاب الطهارة
119 أخرجه البخاري في : كتاب الصلاة ومسلم في : كتاب الصلاة
120 أخرجه الطبراني
121 أخرجه مسلم في : كتاب الصلاة
122 أخرجه الترمذي في : أبواب الصلاة
123 أخرجه الترمذي في : أبواب الصلاة وابن ماجة في : كتاب الصلاة
124 أخرجه الطبراني
125 أخرجه الترمذي في : أبواب الصلاة وابن ماجة في : كتاب الصلاة وقال الترمذي حديث ضعيف
126 أخرجه الترمذي في : أبواب التفسير
127 أخرجه البخاري في : كتاب الدعوات
128 أخرجه الترمذي في : أبواب الدعوات وقال حديث ضعيف لا يعرف إلا من هذا الوجه
129 أخرجه الترمذي في : أبواب الدعوات
130 أخرجه أبو داؤد وابن ماجة في : كتاب الصلاة
131 أخرجه الترمذي في : أبواب الدعوات
132 أخرجه أحمد في المسند

SELECT BIBLIOGRAPHY

ʿAlī, ʿAbdullāh Yūsuf. *The Holy Qur'ān: English Translation of the Meanings and Commentary*. Revised and Edited by the Presidency of Islamic Researches, Ifta, Call and Guidance. Al-Madinah al-Munawwarah, Saudi Arabia.

al-Aṣbaḥī, Mālik ibn Anas. *Al-Muwaṭṭā'*. Multan, Pakistan: Maktaba Fārūqiyya.

al-Bukhārī, Muḥammad ibn Ismāʿīl. *Al-Jāmiʿ al-Ṣaḥīḥ*. Karachi, Pakistan: Qadīmī Kutub Khānā.

Elyas, Afzal Hoosen. *Nawafil*. South Africa.

al-Ḥākim al-Naysābūrī, Muḥammad ibn ʿAbdillāh. *Al-Mustadrak ʿalā 'l-Ṣaḥīḥayn*. Beirut, Lebanon: Dār al-Maʿrifa.

Ibn Abī Shayba, ʿAbdullāh. *Al-Kitāb al-Muṣannaf fi 'l-Ḥadīth wa 'l-Āthār*. Second edition. Bombay, India: Dār al-Salafiyya, 1399/1979.

al-Jazrī, Shams al-Dīn Muḥammad ibn Muḥammad. *Al-Ḥiṣn al-Ḥaṣīn*. Lenasia, South Africa: Islamic Publications.

Lane, E. W. *Arabic-English Lexicon*. Cambridge, England: Islamic Text Society.

al-Nasā'ī, Abū ʿAbd al-Raḥmān Aḥmad ibn Shuʿayb. *Al-Sunan al-Ṣughrā (al-Mujtabā)*. Karachi, Pakistan: Qadīmī Kutub Khānā.

al-Nawawī, Abū Zakariyya Yaḥyā ibn Sharaf. *Al-Adhkār al-Muntakhab min Kalām Sayyid al-Abrār*. First edition. Beirut, Lebanon: Dār al-Khayr, 1411/1990.

al-Naysābūrī, Muslim ibn al-Ḥajjāj. *Al-Ṣaḥīḥ*. Karachi, Pakistan: Qadīmī Kutub Khānā.

al-Qārī, Mullā ʿAlī. *Al-Ḥizb al-Aʿẓam*. Johannersburg, South Africa: Waterval Islamic Institute.

al-Qazwīnī, Abū ʿAbdillāh Muḥammad ibn Yazīd ibn Māja. *Al-Sunan*. Karachi, Pakistan: Qadīmī Kutub Khānā.

al-Ṣanʿānī, ʿAbd al-Razzāq. *Al-Muṣannaf*. First edition. Beirut, Lebanon: al-Majlis al-ʿIlmī, 1390/1970.

al-Sijistānī, Abū Dāwūd Sulaymān ibn al-Ashʿath. *Al-Sunan*. Multan, Pakistan: Maktaba Ḥaqqāniyya.

al-Tirmidhī, Abū ʿĪsā Muḥammad ibn ʿĪsā. *Al-Sunan [al-Jāmiʿ]*. Karachi, Pakistan: Saʿīd Company Limited.

Our Publications

Prayers for Forgiveness

The Path to Perfection

Sufism & Good Character

The Differences of the Imāms

Provisions for the Seekers

Saviours of Islamic Spirit (*Tārīkh-i Daʿwat wa ʿAẓīmat*)

Ghazālī's The Beginning of Guidance (*Bidāyat al-Hidāya*)

Reflections of Pearls

Fiqh al-Imam: Key Proofs in Hanafi Fiqh

The Islamic Laws of Animal Slaughter

Absolute Essentials of Islam

Ṣalāt & Salām: A Manual of Blessings on Allāh's Beloved

Imām Abū Ḥanīfa's *Al-Fiqh al-Akbar* Explained

Ascent to Felicity (*Marāqī 'l-Saʿādāt*)

The Book of Wisdoms (*Ikmāl al-Shiyam*)

Birth Control & Abortion in Islam

The Shāfiʿī Manual of Purity, Prayer & Fasting

Al-Ḥizb al-Aʿẓam (The Supreme Daily Remembrance)

Handbook of a Healthy Muslim Marriage

White Thread
PRESS

www.whitethreadpress.com